CONSTITUTIONAL REFORM ACT 2005

EXPLANATORY NOTES

INTRODUCTION

1.   These explanatory notes relate to the Constitutional Reform Act 2005 which received Royal Assent on 24 March 2005. They have been prepared by the Department for Constitutional Affairs in order to assist the reader in understanding the Act. They do not form part of the Act and have not been endorsed by Parliament.

2.   The notes need to be read in conjunction with the Act. They are not, and are not meant to be, a comprehensive description of the Act. So where a section or part of a section does not seem to require any explanation or comment, none is given.

OVERVIEW

3.   The Constitutional Reform Act modifies the office of Lord Chancellor and makes changes to the way in which some of the functions vested in that office are to be exercised. The Act also creates the Supreme Court of the United Kingdom and abolishes the appellate jurisdiction of the House of Lords. It creates the Judicial Appointments Commission to select people for judicial appointments in England and Wales, and provides for judicial discipline in England and Wales. The Act modifies the jurisdiction of the Judicial Committee of the Privy Council and removes the right of the Lord President of the Council to sit judicially.

4.   The explanatory notes are divided into parts reflecting the structure of the Act. In relation to each Part, there is a summary and background section. Commentary on particular sections is then set out in number order, with the commentary on the various schedules included with the section to which they relate.

5.   Notes on the effects of the Act on: public expenditure; public sector manpower; cost to business and regulatory impact, follow the commentary on sections, as does a brief note on issues relating to the European Convention on Human Rights.

6.   The Act is divided into 7 parts:

Part 1: The Rule of Law

- Part 1: provides that the Act does not adversely affect the Rule of Law or the Lord Chancellor's role in relation to that principle.

Part 2: Arrangements to modify the office of Lord Chancellor

- Part 2: Makes provision for modifying the office of Lord Chancellor so that the office-holder is no longer a judge nor exercises any judicial functions. It also sets out the qualifications for appointment to the office of Lord Chancellor. This Part also deals with functions relating to the judiciary and courts so that they are appropriately shared between the reformed ministerial office of Lord Chancellor and the Lord Chief Justice (and/or other senior members of the judiciary as appropriate). It also provides a guarantee of continued judicial independence. There are provisions in relation to the Speakership of the House of Lords. There are also provisions for the modification, abolition or transfer of other existing functions of the Lord Chancellor and provision that certain functions cannot be transferred from the Lord Chancellor to other Ministers by a Transfer of Functions Order under the Ministers of the Crown Act 1975.

Part 3: The Supreme Court

- Part 3: Makes provisions for a Supreme Court to replace the existing system of Law Lords operating as a committee of the House of Lords. It provides for the appointment of judges to the new Court, the Court's jurisdiction, its procedures, resources (including accommodation) and other matters.

Part 4: Judicial appointments and discipline

- Part 4: Makes provision for a Judicial Appointments Commission to be responsible for recruiting and selecting judges for the Courts of England and Wales and members of certain tribunals, and makes special arrangements for the appointment of the Lord Chief Justice and other Heads of Division and of the Lords Justices of Appeal. It provides for the Commission to report to the Lord Chancellor on who has been selected, and for the Lord Chancellor to make the appointment or the recommendation for appointment to The Queen. It also makes provision for a Judicial Appointments and Conduct Ombudsman, and for judicial discipline.

Part 5: Judicial appointments and removals: Northern Ireland

- Part 5 makes provision about the supply of information to the existing Northern Ireland Judicial Appointments Commission, creates a Northern Ireland Judicial Appointments Ombudsman, and provides a mechanism for the removal of judicial office holders in Northern Ireland. By virtue of section 147(2), Part 5 extends only to Northern Ireland.

Part 6: Other provisions relating to the judiciary

- Part 6: Makes provision regarding Parliamentary disqualification of certain judges; and makes amendments about the Judicial Committee of the Privy Council.

Part 7: General

- Part 7: Restricts the disclosure of confidential information obtained under certain provisions of the Act; makes provision about the interpretation of certain expressions used in the Act, including "enactment" and "subordinate legislation"; confers power to make supplementary provision by order; sets out the procedure for making orders and regulations under the Act; makes minor and consequential amendments and repeals and revocations; and makes provision about the extent, commencement and short title of the Act.

7. Parts 2 and 4 are intended to give substantial effect to the agreement between the Lord Chief Justice of England and Wales and the Lord Chancellor on the proposals relating to the transfer of the Lord Chancellor's judiciary-related functions. This was set out in a document called "Constitutional Reform. The Lord Chancellor's judiciary-related functions: Proposals" (usually referred to as the 'Concordat'). This was placed in the libraries of both Houses of Parliament at the time of the Oral Statement made to the House of Lords by the Lord

Chancellor, and repeated in the House of Commons, on 26th January 2004. The text was also printed as Appendix 6 to the House of Lords Select Committee's Report on the Bill.

PART 1: THE RULE OF LAW

8. Part 1 provides that the Act does not adversely affect the existing constitutional principle of the Rule of Law or the Lord Chancellor's existing constitutional role in relation to that principle.

PART 2: ARRANGEMENTS TO MODIFY THE OFFICE OF LORD CHANCELLOR

SUMMARY

9. Part 2 modifies the office of Lord Chancellor and provides for the future exercise of certain functions of that office and for continued judicial independence. It provides:

(a) that in appointing a person to be Lord Chancellor the Prime Minister must be satisfied that the person is qualified for the post by relevant experience;

(b) that the Lord Chancellor must take a specified oath, in addition to the other oaths required of Ministers;

(c) a guarantee of continued judicial independence in England and Wales, and (separately) in Northern Ireland;

(d) for general statutory responsibilities of the Lord Chief Justice, who will assume the new additional titles of President of the Courts of England and Wales and Head of the Judiciary of England and Wales;

(e) that the most senior Judge within the three legal jurisdictions of the UK (England & Wales, Scotland and Northern Ireland) may make written representations to Parliament on justice-related matters;

(f) for new offices of the Head and Deputy Head of Criminal Justice and Head and Deputy Head of Family Justice;

(g) for the transfer of certain of the Lord Chancellor's statutory functions relating to the judiciary to the Lord Chief Justice (and/or other senior members of the judiciary as appropriate), and for consultation or concurrence between them in the exercise of such functions to reflect the agreement set out in the 'Concordat';

(h) for the amendment of certain statutory provisions that refer to the Lord Chancellor in his capacity as Speaker of the House of Lords, so that they will in future refer to the Speaker of the House of Lords in general terms;

(i) for the modification, transfer and abolition of existing functions of the Lord Chancellor created or modified in primary legislation since the introduction of the Act, and in secondary legislation, local or private acts, charters and other prerogative instruments; and

(j) for the amendment of the Ministers of the Crown Act 1975 to disapply section 1 of that Act to specified functions of the Lord Chancellor, so that they cannot be transferred to another Minister of the Crown by an order under that Act.

BACKGROUND

10. The office of Lord Chancellor is currently both a ministerial and a judicial office. In the main, ministerial powers currently exercisable by the Lord Chancellor that do not relate to the judiciary or the administration of the courts are not affected by the Act. However, some of the Lord Chancellor's functions have been exercised in his capacity as 'Head of the Judiciary' (although this has not historically been a formal or statutory title). Other functions, statutory and otherwise, are currently exercisable by the Lord Chancellor in relation to the judiciary or to the Lord Chancellor's judicial role. The Act ends the judicial role of the Lord Chancellor and precludes the office-holder from holding judicial office. It also modifies the Lord Chancellor's judiciary-related functions in line with the Concordat (see "Overview", above).

11. Section 15 and Schedule 4 provide for judiciary-related functions currently vested in the Lord Chancellor to be transferred to another office holder or otherwise disposed of, and for the modification of certain other functions of the Lord Chancellor. Some of the judiciary-related functions are transferred to the Lord Chief Justice or to another member of the senior judiciary. In many instances, as appropriate to the nature of a particular function, the Lord Chancellor will be required to consult, or obtain the concurrence of, the Lord Chief Justice (or vice versa) before exercising the function. In others, functions may be exercised by the Lord Chancellor or the Lord Chief Justice acting alone. The division of functions into these categories is intended to reflect the principles set out in the Concordat referred to in paragraph 7 above, which are summarised in paragraph 36 below. While the Lord Chief Justice is named as having a role in exercising many of these functions, the Act enables him to delegate any of his functions to holders of other judicial offices, except those functions relating to removals from judicial office. The Act also provides a role for the Lord Chief Justice of Northern Ireland and the Lord President of the Court of Session as appropriate for functions that extend to the jurisdictions of Northern Ireland and Scotland.

12. Statutory provisions that refer to the Lord Chancellor in his capacity as Speaker of the House of Lords are amended by the Act so that they refer to the Speaker of the House of Lords in general terms, rather than the Lord Chancellor. It is a matter for the House of Lords itself to determine any changes to the current arrangements for the office of its Speaker.

13. Section 19 of the Act also makes provision for the transfer, modification and abolition of other functions of the Lord Chancellor, for example those in local and private acts, not yet identified, or functions created by legislation passed in the 2003-04 or 2004-05 Sessions or in secondary legislation. The section also provides a power to amend charters and other prerogative instruments to take account of the reform of the office of the Lord Chancellor. In addition, section 20 of the Act will ensure that certain protected functions (set out in Schedule 7) may not be transferred away from the office of Lord Chancellor by an order under the Ministers of the Crown Act 1975. Section 21 provides for further functions to be added to Schedule 7 (although functions will not be able to be removed from the Schedule by secondary legislation).

COMMENTARY ON SECTIONS

Qualifications for office of Lord Chancellor

Section 2: Lord Chancellor to be qualified by experience

14. Section 2 provides that a person may not be recommended for appointment as Lord Chancellor unless he appears to the Prime Minister to be qualified by experience. Relevant experience for this purpose could include experience as a Minister of the Crown, or as a Member of either House of Parliament. Experience as a qualifying legal practitioner or as a teacher of law in a University could also be taken into account, as could any other experience considered by the Prime Minister to be relevant.

Continued judicial independence

Section 3: Guarantee of continued judicial independence

15. Section 3 places a duty on Ministers of the Crown (including the Lord Chancellor), and all others with responsibility for matters relating to the judiciary or otherwise to the administration of justice to uphold the continued independence of the judiciary. It also sets out two particular duties that are to be exercised for the purpose of upholding that independence.

16. The first is a duty on Ministers of the Crown not to seek to influence particular judicial decisions through any special access to the judiciary. "Special access" is intended to refer to any access over and above that which might be exercised by a member of the general public. So the duty does not, for example, limit what may be said on a Minister's behalf in court in the course of presenting a case to the court in the usual way.

17. The second duty requires the Lord Chancellor to have regard to the need to defend the continued independence of the judiciary, the need for the judiciary to have proper support necessary to enable them to exercise their functions, and the need for the public interest in matters relating to the judiciary or otherwise to the administration of justice to be properly represented in decisions affecting those matters. This section should be read in conjunction with Part 1 of the Courts Act 2003, which sets out the duty of the Lord Chancellor to ensure that there is an efficient and effective system to support the carrying on of the business of the courts of England and Wales.

Section 4: Guarantee of continued judicial independence: Northern Ireland

18. Section 4 substitutes a new section 1 of the Justice (Northern Ireland) Act 2002 to ensure that the provision made by that Act in relation to Northern Ireland is consistent with the provision made in section 3 of the Constitutional Reform Act.

19. Section 1 of the 2002 Act, which has not yet been commenced, already contains provision designed to place those with responsibility for the administration of justice in Northern Ireland under a duty to uphold the continued independence of the judiciary. The new section 1 specifies and extends the range of persons upon whom the duty is imposed. Under the new section, the First Minister, the deputy First Minister, Northern Ireland Ministers and anyone with responsibility for the judiciary or the administration of justice specific to Northern Ireland, will be subject to the duty to uphold judicial independence. The new section will also provide that in upholding judicial independence, Ministers must not seek to interfere with particular judicial decisions through any special access to the judiciary. The duties imposed

by section 1 have UK wide territorial extent and include the judiciary throughout the United Kingdom.

Representations by senior judges

Section 5: Representations to Parliament

20. Section 5 provides that the Lord Chief Justice of England and Wales, the Lord Chief Justice of Northern Ireland and the Lord President of the Court of Session may table written representations to Parliament on matters relating to the judiciary or the administration of justice. In respect of the Lord President of the Court of Session and the Lord Chief Justice of Northern Ireland, this function is qualified by subsections (2) and (3) in order to respect the devolution settlements with Scotland and Northern Ireland respectively.

Section 6: Representations to the Northern Ireland Assembly

21. Section 6 makes provision for the Lord Chief Justice of Northern Ireland to lay written representations before the Northern Ireland Assembly on matters relating to the judiciary, or to the administration of justice in Northern Ireland. The Lord Chief Justice may make such representations if they relate to excepted or reserved matters to which a Bill for an Act of the Assembly relates; or to transferred matters, unless they are transferred matters to which a Bill for an Act of Parliament relates.

The Judiciary and the Courts in England and Wales

Section 7: President of the Courts of England and Wales

22. Section 7 provides a new, additional, statutory title of President of the Courts of England and Wales for the Lord Chief Justice. This section also recognises that the Lord Chief Justice is the Head of the Judiciary of England and Wales.

23. The section sets out the responsibilities of the President of the Courts of England and Wales. It also sets out the courts to which the presidency applies. In his role as President of the Courts of England and Wales, the Lord Chief Justice is to be responsible for representing the views of the judiciary of England and Wales to Parliament, the Lord Chancellor and Ministers of the Crown generally. He is also to be responsible, within the resources made available by the Lord Chancellor, for maintaining appropriate arrangements for the welfare, training and guidance of the judiciary of England and Wales, and for maintaining appropriate arrangements for the deployment of the judiciary of England and Wales and allocating work within courts. In relation to the issue of deployment, it should be noted that the Lord Chief Justice will also have a role in the appointment of judicial office holders to committees, boards and similar bodies, as set out in paragraphs 46-49 of the 'Concordat'; his role in such appointments so far as governed by statute is provided for by amendments made by Schedule 4.

Section 8: Head and Deputy Head of Criminal Justice

24. Section 8 creates a new statutory post of Head of Criminal Justice, which will be held ex officio by the Lord Chief Justice of England and Wales or, after consultation with the Lord Chancellor , by his nominee. This section also provides that the Lord Chief Justice may appoint a Deputy Head of Criminal Justice. The creation of these new posts mirrors the existing statutory posts of Head and Deputy Head of Civil Justice, established by section 62 of the Courts Act 2003.

Section 9: Head and Deputy Head of Family Justice

25. Section 9 creates a new statutory post of Head of Family Justice, which will be held ex officio by the President of the Family Division. This section also provides that the Lord Chief Justice may appoint a Deputy Head of Family Justice. The creation of these new posts mirrors the existing statutory posts of Head and Deputy Head of Civil Justice, established by section 62 of the Courts Act 2003.

Judiciary and Courts in Northern Ireland

Section 10: The Lord Chancellor and Northern Ireland Courts

26. Section 10 provides for a new section to be inserted into the Judicature (Northern Ireland) Act 1978, corresponding to section 1 of the Courts Act 2003. It places a statutory duty on the Lord Chancellor to ensure there is an efficient and effective system to support the Supreme Court of Northern Ireland and the county courts, magistrates' courts and coroners' courts in Northern Ireland and to ensure that appropriate services are provided for those courts. It also requires the Lord Chancellor to lay before Parliament a report as to the way in which this duty has been discharged.

Section 11: Lord Chief Justice of Northern Ireland

27. At present, the Lord Chief Justice of Northern Ireland is President of the Court of Appeal, High Court, and Crown Court but has no role in relation to the county courts or the magistrates' courts. Section 12 of the Justice (Northern Ireland) Act 2002 Act provides for the Lord Chief Justice to be president of the Court of Appeal, Crown Court, High Court, county courts and magistrates' courts and head of the judges and magistrates who sit in them. It does not, however, bestow any formal title.

28. Section 11 amends section 12(1) of the Justice (Northern Ireland) Act 2002 to take account of reform of the office of the Lord Chancellor. It provides for a new statutory office and title of President of the Courts of Northern Ireland to be assumed by the Lord Chief Justice of Northern Ireland. It also provides for the Lord Chief Justice of Northern Ireland to be Head of the Judiciary of Northern Ireland.

29. The section sets out the responsibilities of the President of the Courts of Northern Ireland and the courts to which the presidency applies. The responsibilities, which are broadly similar to those of the Lord Chief Justice of England and Wales under section 7 of the Act, are:

- representing the views of the judiciary of Northern Ireland to Parliament, the Lord Chancellor and Ministers of the Crown generally;

- representing the views of the judiciary of Northern Ireland to the Northern Ireland Assembly, the First Minister and deputy First Minister and Northern Ireland Ministers;

- maintaining appropriate arrangements for the welfare, training and guidance of the judiciary of Northern Ireland within the resources made available by the Lord Chancellor; and

- maintaining appropriate arrangements for the deployment of the judiciary of Northern Ireland and the allocation of work within the courts.

Other provisions about the judiciary and courts

Section 12 and Schedule 1: Powers to make rules

30. Section 12 introduces Schedule 1, which deals with powers to make rules of court that are currently vested in the Lord Chancellor alone, rather than in a rule Committee. By virtue of these provisions, the rules will now be made by the Lord Chief Justice with the concurrence of the Lord Chancellor. Part 1 of Schedule 1 sets out the procedure by which the rules will now be made. Part 2 of the Schedule amends the statutes which confer the rule-making powers so as to incorporate the new procedure.

31.. The requirement that the Lord Chancellor should concur with any rules made by the Lord Chief Justice mirrors the existing statutory powers of the Lord Chancellor to allow or disallow rules made by rule committees. A new power to direct that the Lord Chief Justice make rules to achieve a specified purpose is vested in the Lord Chancellor. Again, this mirrors the situation for rules made by rule committees which are dealt with in Schedule 4 to the Act. In relation to certain family procedure rules, the procedure under part 1 of Schedule 1 to the Act will only have temporary effect, until sections 75 to 80 of the Courts Act 2003 are brought into effect and the Family Procedure Rule Committee is established.

Section 13 and Schedule 2: Powers to Give Directions

32. Section 13 introduces Schedule 2, which deals with powers to give directions that are currently vested in the Lord Chancellor. By virtue of these provisions, the directions will now be given by the Lord Chief Justice, generally with the concurrence of the Lord Chancellor. Part 1 of Schedule 2 sets out the procedure by which the directions will now be given. Part 2 of the Schedule amends the statutes which confer the direction-giving powers so as to incorporate the new procedure. The Lord Chief Justice may, with the approval of the Lord Chancellor, delegate his functions under the new procedure; the expectation is that the powers would usually be delegated to the Head of Criminal, Civil or Family Justice (as appropriate). The new procedure is similar to that which will apply to the rules dealt with in section 12 and Schedule 1 (see paragraphs 30 and 31 above).

33. The concurrence of the Lord Chancellor is not needed for directions concerning guidance as to the application or interpretation of the law or the making of judicial decisions. Nor is the Lord Chancellor's concurrence needed for directions that relate to criteria for determining which judges may be allocated to hear particular categories of case; but the Lord Chancellor must be consulted before such directions are given.

Section 14 and Schedule 3: Transfer of appointment functions to Her Majesty

34. Section 14 introduces Schedule 3, which provides that appointments to the judicial offices listed will in future be made by Her Majesty The Queen rather than the Lord Chancellor as currently. Paragraph 1 of the Schedule transfers to Her Majesty the power under section 6 of the County Courts Act 1984 to appoint civil District Judges to county courts and gives the Lord Chief Justice the power to assign them to their districts. It also provides that their salaries shall be determined by the Lord Chancellor with the concurrence of the Treasury, and may not be reduced. This protection brings civil District Judges more closely into line with District Judges (Magistrates' Courts) and with more senior members of the judiciary. Paragraph 2 makes corresponding provision for the assignment of civil District Judges to District Registries of the High Court. Paragraph 3 transfers to Her Majesty the power to

appoint High Court Masters and Registrars, and re-enacts with amendments the qualifications for appointment or promotion to the posts of the senior High Court Masters and Registrars. The table in paragraph 3(4) refers to the qualifying office for appointment as Senior District Judge of the Family Division as 'Registrar of the Principal Registry of the Family Division'. This office was renamed 'District Judge of the Principal Registry of the Family Division' by the Courts and Legal Services Act 1990, and the reference is to that office. Paragraphs 5 and 6 transfer to Her Majesty the power to appoint the Senior District Judge (Chief Magistrate).

35. All of these offices are also listed in Schedule 14, and appointments will in future be made by Her Majesty on the advice of the Lord Chancellor, after selection by the Judicial Appointments Commission.

Section 15 and Schedules 4 and 5: Other functions of the Lord Chancellor and organisation of the Courts

36. Section 15 introduces Schedule 4 which provides for the transfer of certain functions of the Lord Chancellor and the modification of other functions of the Lord Chancellor (including those functions that he exercises in relation to Northern Ireland under legislation with UK wide extent). The modified functions will, in general, now be exercised with either the concurrence of, or after consultation with, the Lord Chief Justice of England and Wales or another senior judge, as appropriate. Provision is made for some of those functions that are transferred away from the Lord Chancellor to be exercised either with the concurrence of, or after consultation with, the Lord Chancellor. Section 15 also introduces Schedule 5 which makes similar provision for functions that the Lord Chancellor exercises under legislation relating to Northern Ireland.

37. Schedule 4 makes the amendments referred to in section 15 by modifying enactments containing or relating to the functions in question. The effect of the amendments made by this Schedule may be summarised as follows:

- The existing statutory functions of the Lord Chancellor that relate to the following matters in England and Wales will be transferred to the Lord Chief Justice: (i) the posting and roles of individual judges within the framework of the court system; (ii) the responsibility to make rules relating to deployment of magistrates; (iii) the authorisation and assignment of judges, allocation of work and the distribution of business within the same level of the court system, (e.g. between divisions of the High Court); and (iv) the nomination of judges to deal with specific areas of business and to fill judicial leadership posts such as the Presiding Judges.

- The existing statutory functions of the Lord Chancellor that enable him to determine the framework for the appointment of judicial office holders to committees, boards and similar bodies in England and Wales will remain with the Lord Chancellor, while the statutory functions that enable him to appoint individual judges to such bodies will be transferred to the Lord Chief Justice.

- As regards the making of court rules in respect of England and Wales, where statutory committees presently exist, the relevant provisions will be modified to take account of the division of the Lord Chancellor's functions between him and the Lord Chief Justice. The appointment of non-judicial members of rule committees will continue to be made by the Lord Chancellor and judicial members will be appointed by the

Lord Chief Justice. In addition, there will be a new power for the Lord Chancellor to require rule committees to change rules or to make new rules to achieve a specified purpose, and to allow rules made by such committees. He may disallow rules but is required to provide written reasons. (See section 12 and Schedule 1 for rule making powers not related to rule making committees.)

- Statutory references to the Vice-Chancellor are amended to provide for the new title of "Chancellor of the High Court". Statutory references within the Courts Act 2003 relating to the Head of Civil Justice are amended to bring them in line with the positions of Head of Criminal Justice and Head of Family Justice in sections 8 and 9 of the Act. A new position of "President of the Queen's Bench Division" is also created; this post will not be held by the Lord Chief Justice, but by a separate office holder who will be a Head of Division in his own right.

- The Lord Chief Justice will replace the Lord Chancellor as the office holder before whom judges in England and Wales will take their oaths. The Lord Chief Justice will take his oath before the Master of the Rolls, the President of the Queen's Bench Division, the President of the Family Division and the Chancellor of the High Court (formerly the Vice-Chancellor).

- Certain existing statutory functions of the Lord Chancellor are now to be exercised only with the concurrence of, or after consultation with, the Lord Chief Justice of England and Wales. Where the function relates not only to England and Wales, but also to Northern Ireland or Scotland (or both), an equivalent concurring or consultative role has been provided for the Lord Chief Justice of Northern Ireland or the Lord President of the Court of Session (as appropriate). In addition, where the Lord Chancellor exercises an appointment or removal function in relation to an officer who sits wholly or mainly in Northern Ireland or Scotland, the Schedule provides that he must either consult with, or seek the concurrence of, the Lord Chief Justice of Northern Ireland or the Lord President of the Court of Session (as appropriate).

- Where amendments are made to other Acts by the Schedule to confer functions on the Lord Chief Justice of England and Wales, the Lord Chief Justice of Northern Ireland or the Lord President of the Court of Session, a provision is added in each case permitting them to delegate the function to another judicial office-holder, except where the function relates to removals from judicial office. In the case of the Lord Chief Justice of England and Wales, the function may be delegated to any "judicial office holder", as defined in section 109 of the Act. These are the Master of the Rolls, the President of the Queen's Bench Division, the President of the Family Division, the Chancellor of the High Court, a Lord Justice of Appeal, a puisne judge of the High Court and the holder of any office listed in Schedule 14 to the Act. In the case of the Lord Chief Justice of Northern Ireland the function may be delegated to the holder of any office listed in Schedule 1 to the Justice (Northern Ireland) Act 2002 or to a Lord Justice of Appeal. In the case of the Lord President of the Court of Session, the function may be delegated to any judge of the Court of Session who is a member of the First or Second Division of the Inner House of that Court.

- All of this means that the following statutory functions will remain with the Lord Chancellor: (i) those concerning the framework for the organisation of the courts system, including setting the geographical and jurisdictional boundaries within England and Wales; (ii) the provision and allocation of financial, material and human resources for the administration of justice; (iii) those relating to the pay, pensions and terms and conditions of the judiciary and the provision of staff and resources for training of the judiciary; and (iv) the determination of the overall number of judges and the distribution of business between different levels of courts in England and Wales;

38. Schedule 4 includes provisions preliminary to the making of arrangements for ending the Lord Chancellor's ecclesiastical patronage and, as announced by the Government on 2 March 2004, for its future exercise by the Prime Minister. These changes will be completed by non-legislative means. Schedule 4 also transfers the Lord Chancellor's functions in relation to appeals under section 11 of the Ecclesiastical Licences Act 1533 and section 5 of the Public Notaries Act 1843 to the Chancellor of the High Court.

39. Schedule 4 further provides that the Lord Chancellor's power (with the concurrence of HM Treasury) under section 14 of the Local Land Charges Act 1975 to set fees for local land charges will, with the exception of fees for personal searches, be devolved to registering authorities in England. Registering authorities are defined by section 3 of the 1975 Act and include most local authorities. Each registering authority in England will be required to set fees for the local land charge services they provide. Registering authorities will be able to set a fee for each service, description of service or group of services which recovers up to, but not more than, their costs of delivering that service. These fees must be published shortly before the beginning of every financial year and before the date the local authority sets for any changes to take effect. In setting and publishing fees, registering authorities will have to have regard to such guidance as the Lord Chancellor may issue, which guidance will be laid before both Houses of Parliament.

40. Schedule 5 transfers some of the Lord Chancellor's functions to the Lord Chief Justice of Northern Ireland. In some cases the concurrence of, or consultation with, the Lord Chancellor is required before the Lord Chief Justice may exercise the function. Schedule 5 also modifies some of the Lord Chancellor's functions to provide the Lord Chief Justice with a consultative or concurring role. The Schedule enables the Lord Chief Justice to delegate functions transferred to him by the Act (where there is no existing power of delegation) to other office holders to ensure flexibility and that the Lord Chief Justice can continue to fulfil his primary role as a judge. (The office holders to whom these functions may be delegated are the same as those referred to in relation to Schedule 4: the holder of any office listed in Schedule 1 to the Justice (Northern Ireland) Act 2002 or a Lord Justice of Appeal.)

41. The Schedule provides that the Lord Chancellor, in consultation with the Lord Chief Justice of Northern Ireland, will be responsible for setting the organisational framework of the court system, the destination and allocation of proceedings and for providing resources for the administration of judges. The Lord Chief Justice will be responsible for sitting times and places of courts, the assignment and authorisation of judges and the distribution of business within the same level of court. The Lord Chief Justice, after consultation with the Lord Chancellor, will be responsible for nominating to various posts and providing judicial training.

42. The Lord Chancellor's functions of appointing members, or judicial members, of rule committees are transferred by the Schedule to the Lord Chief Justice, with a consultation role in relation to the appointment of non-judicial members for the Lord Chancellor. Provisions relating to rules made by a Committee are also amended to provide the Lord Chancellor with a power to require rules committees to make rules to achieve a specified purpose. There is also a requirement on the Lord Chancellor to provide written reasons in the event that he disallows rules made by a rules committee. The Lord Chancellor's function of making rules without a committee is, in general, to continue to be exercised by the Lord Chancellor but with a consultation role for the Lord Chief Justice.

43. The Justice (Northern Ireland) Act 2002 provides the framework for appointments in Northern Ireland, in particular for the establishment of a Judicial Appointments Commission for Northern Ireland, which will be established in June this year. This Schedule does not alter those arrangements other than to make a number of technical amendments or to correct anomalies. In particular, it brings a number of judicial appointments within the scope of the Northern Ireland Judicial Appointments Commission and makes a number of amendments to take account of changes flowing from the reform of the office of the Lord Chancellor, for example, prescribing qualification requirements.

44. The Schedule also provides for the repeal of certain functions of the Lord Chancellor, which are now redundant.

Section 16: Functions of the Lord Chief Justice during vacancy or incapacity

45. Section 16 provides that if there is a vacancy in the office of Lord Chief Justice, or if he is incapacitated, the functions of the Lord Chief Justice may be exercised by the Master of the Rolls or the next most senior Head of Division, as set out in subsection (3). If any of these offices are themselves vacant the functions may be exercised by the next most senior Head of Division as specified in the section. Any decision as to whether the Lord Chief Justice is incapacitated, or has ceased to be incapacitated, must be agreed in writing by at least three of the four Heads of Division.

Lord Chancellor's Oath

Section 17: Lord Chancellor's Oath

46. Section 17 amends the Promissory Oaths Act 1868 to provide for a new oath to be taken by the Lord Chancellor. The terms of the oath refer to the Lord Chancellor's roles in relation to the independence of the judiciary, the rule of law and supporting the running of the courts. It will be taken alongside the existing oath of allegiance and official oath (see sections 2 and 3 of the 1868 Act) upon taking up office. As the Lord Chancellor is no longer a judge, he will no longer take the judicial oath (see section 4 of the 1868 Act).

Speakership of the House of Lords

Section 18 and Schedule 6: Speakership of the House of Lords

47. Section 18 introduces Schedule 6. Schedule 6 provides that references in primary legislation to the Lord Chancellor in his capacity as Speaker of the House of Lords are replaced with references to the 'Speaker of the House of Lords'. This change will ensure that the provisions amended are capable of applying to any Speaker of that House, who need not however be known formally by that title. The purpose of the provision is to enable the House

of Lords to decide upon future arrangements for its Speakership without the need to amend existing references in primary legislation.

Supplementary

Section 19: Transfer, modification or abolition of functions by order

48. Section 19 gives the Lord Chancellor power to do any of the following things by order: to transfer, modify or abolish an existing function of his office; to provide for such a function to be exercised concurrently with another person; or to provide that such a function that is exercisable concurrently with another person ceases to be so exercisable. Subsection (2) makes it clear that such an order can, if necessary, amend or repeal other enactments, subordinate legislation, and other instruments or documents. The power does not apply in respect of functions of the Lord Chancellor that are listed in Schedule 7 to the Act.

49. This power extends wider than the power to transfer ministerial functions under the Ministers of the Crown Act 1975. There are two main differences compared with the power in the 1975 Act: the new power is not restricted to the transfer of functions to other Ministers; and the new power also allows for the modification or abolition of a function. The new power also extends wider than the power to make supplementary provision in section 143 of the Constitutional Reform Act 2005. The power in section 143 may only be used if the Lord Chancellor considers it necessary or expedient for the purposes of, in consequence of, or for giving full effect to, any provision of the Act. There is no such restriction on the power under section 19.

50. An order under section 19 is subject to affirmative resolution procedure in any case where it amends a public general act and in most cases where it amends subordinate legislation which was itself subject to affirmative resolution procedure (see section 144(5)(b) and (c) of the Act). In any other case an order under section 19 is subject to negative resolution procedure. .

51. One of the purposes of this power is to ensure that effect may be given to the Concordat agreed with the Lord Chief Justice (see paragraph 7 above), in particular with regard to functions set out in legislation (whether primary or secondary) made during, or soon after, the passage of the Constitutional Reform Bill through Parliament. (The power is limited to amending legislation made in, or under, Acts passed up to and including in the session in which this Act is enacted). These provisions are also intended to be used in relation to, for example, functions of the Lord Chancellor conferred by private, personal or local Acts which may have been missed and thus have not been addressed in the substantive provisions of the Act. This power is also intended for use in relation to the functions of the Lord Chancellor under charters or other governing instruments of private institutions, such as colleges or universities. Where they wish to alter or remove the role of the Lord Chancellor, this power would avoid the need for each of the institutions concerned to make their own separate arrangements.

52. Where, by an order under this section, a function has been modified or has become exercisable concurrently with another person, the order may also provide for the function to be added to Schedule 7 (Protected Functions of the Minister). The effect of this will be that the power will not thereafter be transferable to another Minister under the Ministers of the Crown Act 1975: see below. This power is intended to avoid the need for a separate order under section 20 of the Act where a function is modified under this section and there is a need

to include it within Schedule 7. It is expected to apply principally to functions of the Lord Chancellor created in primary legislation since the introduction of the Bill.

Schedule 7: Protected Functions of the Lord Chancellor

53.   Schedule 7 lists various protected functions of the Lord Chancellor which may not be transferred to other Ministers by a Transfer of Functions Order under the Ministers of the Crown Act.   These include functions relating to the custody or use of the Great Seal; functions conferred on the Lord Chancellor by the Constitutional Reform Act or modified by that Act; other listed functions; and listed functions in relation to Northern Ireland. The listed functions may not be transferred by an order under section 19 of the Act or by an order under section 1 of the Ministers of the Crown Act 1975 (as amended by section 20 of the Act).

54.   Schedule 7 may be amended so as to include new functions by any of the following. First, an order under section 19 of the Act, if the order provides for a function of the Lord Chancellor to become exercisable concurrently with another person or for a function to be modified (see section 19(7) of the Act). Secondly, a Transfer of Functions Order under section 1 of the Ministers of the Crown Act 1975, if the order provides for a function to be transferred to the Lord Chancellor, to become exercisable by him concurrently with another person, or to remain exercisable by him but to cease to be exercisable by another person (see section 1(7) of the 1975 Act, inserted by section 20(2) of the Constitutional Reform Act 2005). Thirdly, an order under section 21 of the 2005 Act (see below)

Section 20: Protected functions not transferable under Minister of the Crown Act 1975

55.   Section 20 amends sections 1 and 5 of the Ministers of the Crown Act 1975 so that the power to transfer functions under section 1 of that Act does not apply to the functions of the Lord Chancellor specified in Schedule 7. In general, these functions relate to the Great Seal, the judiciary or the organisation of the courts. This will mean that the specified functions cannot be transferred to another Minister by a Transfer of Functions Order under the 1975 Act.

Section 21: Amendment of Schedule 7

56.   Section 21 provides a power for the Lord Chancellor to add statutory functions of the Lord Chancellor (including those exercisable by him concurrently with another person) to Schedule 7. This only applies to statutory functions under legislation passed in the same Session as, or in Sessions prior to, the Session in which the Act was passed. Its principal purpose is to add to Schedule 7 functions of the Lord Chancellor created in primary legislation since the introduction of the Bill for the Constitutional Reform Act.

Section 22: Transfers: supplementary

57.   Section 22 applies where a function of the Lord Chancellor is transferred to another person under the Act itself, or by an order made under section 19. Its purpose is to ensure that there will be a smooth transition when the function is transferred. It therefore provides for the continuing validity of actions relating to the function taken before the transfer.   . References to the Lord Chancellor, his Department or any officer of his Department that occur in Acts or other instruments are to be read as referring to the person who will undertake the function in the future or his department or officers (as appropriate). Legal proceedings involving the Lord Chancellor in relation to a function which is transferred can be continued by or against the person who assumes the function. Printed documents and forms that relate

to a transferred function also continue to be valid despite references to the Lord Chancellor, his Department or his staff. Subsection (2) provides that where Her Majesty will in future perform a function of the Lord Chancellor, the Lord Chancellor will still continue any associated action in relation to that function.

PART 3 THE SUPREME COURT

SUMMARY

58.   Part 3 of the Act creates a Supreme Court of the United Kingdom (which is generally to be known as 'The Supreme Court' in the Act and other legislation) and makes provision for the transfer to the Supreme Court of the appellate jurisdiction of the House of Lords and the devolution jurisdiction of the Judicial Committee of the Privy Council. The new Supreme Court will be separate from Parliament.

BACKGROUND

59.   At present the exercise of the highest level of jurisdiction in the United Kingdom is shared between the Appellate Committee of the House of Lords and the Judicial Committee of the Privy Council. The Appellate Committee of the House of Lords receives appeals from the courts in England and Wales and Northern Ireland, and in civil cases from Scotland. The Judicial Committee of the Privy Council, in addition to its overseas and ecclesiastical jurisdiction, considers questions as to whether the devolved administrations, the Scottish Parliament, the National Assembly for Wales and the Northern Ireland Assembly are acting within their legal powers. Support to the Appellate Committee is provided by the House's administration under the Clerk of the Parliaments. Support for the Judicial Committee is provided by staff supporting the Privy Council.

60.   In addition to the Lords of Appeal in Ordinary certain other holders of high judicial office are also members of the House of Lords. A number of other members of the House of Lords hold other full-time or part-time judicial office and a number of members of the House of Commons hold part-time judicial-office.

61.   The Act seeks to make a distinct constitutional separation between the legislature and the judiciary. It creates a Supreme Court of the United Kingdom giving it the appellate jurisdiction of the House of Lords and the devolution jurisdiction of the Judicial Committee of the Privy Council. It makes provision to allow for the appointment of members of the Court in a way that requires the participation of the judiciary and the devolved administrations throughout the United Kingdom. It makes provision to determine the practices and procedures of the court, to allow the Lord Chancellor to provide staff, equipment, security arrangements and accommodation for the Court. It also makes general provision for the proceedings of the Court to be broadcast in certain circumstances.

62.   As a counterpart to the creation of the Supreme Court the Act restricts the right of members of the House of Lords to sit and vote for so long as they hold full time judicial office. Finally the Act makes consequential and transitional provisions to allow the transfer of functions to the Court.

COMMENTARY ON SECTIONS

Section 23: The Supreme Court

63.   This section establishes the Supreme Court of the United Kingdom, and sets out the composition of the Supreme Court.   It also sets out the method of appointing judges, including the President and Deputy President (the process for selection of persons to be recommended for appointment is to be found in sections 26-31). It also provides for the title of the judges of the Supreme Court other than the President and Deputy President.

64.   Subsection (2) provides both for complement and method of appointment. The Court will comprise 12 judges, who are to be appointed by Her Majesty by letters patent. By virtue of subsection (5), Her Majesty may, also by letters patent, appoint one of the judges to be President and one to be Deputy President. It will be possible for a person to be appointed as President or Deputy President without having first served as a judge of the Supreme Court (see Section 26(4)).

65.   Subsection (3) provides a power for Her Majesty to increase or further increase the number of judges of the Supreme Court by Order in Council. This may only be done, however, if, as set out in subsection (4), a draft of the Order has been laid before and approved by each House of Parliament (that is, by affirmative resolution procedure).

66.   Subsection (6) provides that the judges of the Supreme Court other than the President of the Supreme Court and the Deputy President of the Supreme Court (who will have those titles) will be styled 'Justices of the Supreme Court'.

67.   Subsection (7) provides that the Court will still be properly constituted even if there is a vacancy among the judges of the Court or in the office of President or Deputy President.

Section 24: First members of the Court.

68.   This Section provides for the first judges of the Supreme Court to be the Lords of Appeal in Ordinary holding office at the date of commencement. This is a one-off provision to provide for the transition of members of the Appellate Committee of the House of Lords from the Appellate Committee to the Supreme Court.

69.   The effect of Section 24(a) is that on establishment of the Court (with the commencement of section 23), Lords of Appeal in Ordinary immediately before commencement will become the first Supreme Court judges.

70.   Section 24(b) and (c) make provision for the first holders of the offices of President and Deputy President, providing that the senior Lord of Appeal in Ordinary prior to commencement will become the President and the second senior Lord of Appeal in Ordinary prior to commencement will become the Deputy President of the Court.

Appointment of judges

Section 25: Qualification for Appointment

71.   This Section defines eligibility for appointment as a judge of the Supreme Court, which will be the same as eligibility for appointment as a Lord of Appeal in Ordinary.

72.   Subsection (1) sets out the qualifying requirements for appointment as a Supreme Court judge. There are two separate possible routes to qualification. First, a person is eligible

if he has held high judicial office, as defined in subsections (1) and (2) of section 54, for at least 2 years.

73.   Alternatively, to qualify for appointment as a Supreme Court judge, a person would have to have been a qualifying practitioner for at least 15 years.

74.   Subsection (2) defines "qualifying practitioner" for the purposes of this section .

Section 26: Selection of members of the Court

75.   This section, together with sections 27, 28, 29, 30, and 31 and Schedule 8, provides for the process by which candidates for appointment to the Supreme Court are to be selected and recommended to Her Majesty for appointment.

76.   Subsection (1) sets out the offices to which appointments are to be made by this process.   Subsection (5) provides that the Lord Chancellor must convene a selection commission if there is a vacancy in one of those offices, or if it appears to the Lord Chancellor that there will soon be such a vacancy. Schedule 8, which is introduced by subsection (6), makes provision about the composition of selection commissions. Sections 27 to 29 set out the details of the process to be followed by a selection commission.

77.   At the final stage of that selection process, once sections 27, 28 and 29 (and, if necessary, sections 30 and 31) have been followed, the Lord Chancellor notifies the Prime Minister of the identity of the person selected by the commission. Then, under subsections (2), (3) and (4) of section 26, the Prime Minister must recommend the Queen to appoint the person notified to him by the Lord Chancellor.

Schedule 8: Supreme Court selection commissions

78.   This Schedule contains the rules governing the composition of the selection commission for the appointment of judges to the Supreme Court. It sets out who is eligible to sit on the commission, how it is to be convened, and the rules for its operation. This selection commission will put forward candidates for appointment to the Lord Chancellor, for notification to the Prime Minister and eventual recommendation by the Prime Minister to Her Majesty for appointment, according to the procedure set out in sections 26-31.

Part 1 Selection Commissions

Selection Commission

79.   Paragraph 1 makes provision for the membership of the Supreme Court selection commission which, under section 27, will select one candidate and put forward that candidate to the Lord Chancellor accordingly. The selection commission will consist of the President of the Supreme Court (who, by virtue of Paragraph 7, will chair the commission), the Deputy President of the Supreme Court and one member from each of the territorial appointing commissions (nominated under paragraph 6), one of whom must (by virtue of paragraph 6(3)) be a person who is not legally qualified.

Special rules where President or Deputy President's place unfilled

80.   Paragraphs 2- 4 make provision for the composition of the Selection Commission if the place of the President and / or the Deputy President on the commission is unfilled by reason of one of the situations set out in paragraph 5.

81.   Paragraph 2(2) provides for the next most senior ordinary judge in the Supreme Court to take the unfilled position on the selection commission if either the President or Deputy President is unable to sit. Paragraph 3(2) provides for the most senior ordinary judge and the second most senior ordinary judge to take the unfilled position if both the President and Deputy President are unable to sit.

82.   If the unfilled place or places are not taken in accordance with paragraph 2(2) or paragraph 3(2) (for example because all of the Supreme Court judges wish to be considered for a vacancy that has arisen) then paragraph 2(3) & (4) and paragraph 3(3), (4) & (5) provide for the most senior judiciary from the three jurisdictions of the UK to be members of the commission, unless one of the jurisdictions is already represented through the presence of the President, Deputy President or one of the ordinary judges (for example, if his "home jurisdiction", as defined in paragraph 4, is Scotland, Scotland is represented). In this event only two of the senior judiciary would be required – those from the jurisdictions not already represented (in the example above, from England and Wales and Northern Ireland, since Scotland is represented).

83.   Paragraph 4 provides for the determination of the home jurisdiction of a judge of the Supreme Court. Separate provision is made according to whether the judge in question became a member of the Court by virtue of being a Lord of Appeal in Ordinary at commencement, or was appointed to the Court subsequently, working in the former case by reference to the qualification requirement of the Appellate Jurisdiction Act 1876 (under which Lords of Appeal in Ordinary will have been appointed) rather than those of section 24 of the Act.

Disqualification

84.   Paragraph 5 details the circumstances in which judicial members of the commission are disqualified from sitting on the commission.

85.   Paragraph 5(1) provides for cases of illness or other incapacity: any judge who might be eligible to sit on the appointing commission is considered to be disqualified if the Lord Chancellor believes that the person is for the time being incapacitated from serving on the commission.

86.   Paragraphs 5(2), (3) and (4) provide for cases where a person is a candidate for appointment to the vacancy under consideration: judges of the Supreme Court below the position of President and judges from territorial jurisdictions will be disqualified from membership of the commission unless they first give the Lord Chancellor notice that they do not wish to be considered for the vacancy being filled.

Non-judicial members of the selection commission

87.   Paragraph 6 sets out the rules governing the appointment of members of the territorial appointing commissions to the selection commission.

88.   Under paragraph 6(2), the Lord Chancellor will be responsible for nominating one member of each of the territorial appointing commissions; however, under paragraph 6(4) he may only do this on the recommendation of the territorial appointing commission of which the person is a member. Sub-paragraph (3) provides that at least one of the persons nominated from the territorial appointing commissions must be non-legally qualified (defined for the purposes of this paragraph in paragraph 6(6) and (7)). In effect this means that if at

least one of the territorial commissions does not recommend a non-legally qualified person, the Lord Chancellor will, before the commission can be convened, have to broker a solution with the territorial commissions whereby one of them will agree to recommend a non-legally qualified member.

Chairing of a selection commission

89.　　Paragraph 7 identifies the President of the Supreme Court as the person who shall normally chair the selection commission for the Supreme Court and provides that, if the President is not available, the most senior member of the commission will chair it.

Interpretation

90.　　Paragraph 8 defines for the purpose of this Schedule what is meant by a reference to a selection commission for a particular office. . For example (sub-paragraph (a)): 'Selection commission for the office of President' means a selection commission convened in the case of a vacancy in the office of President.

91.　　Paragraph 9(1) defines for the purposes of Part 1 of this Schedule the meaning of "Judicial Appointments Board for Scotland" and "territorial judge".

92.　　Paragraph 9(2) defines for the purposes of Part 1 of this Schedule how the seniority of judges of the Supreme Court is to be determined (taking account, where appropriate, of seniority "inherited" from service in the House of Lords) and, in relation to the selection commission, how the seniority of the territorial judges appointed under paragraph 2(3) and Paragraph 3(3) & (4) is to be determined.

Part 2 Dissolution

Any Selection commission

93.　　Part 2 of this Schedule sets out the circumstances in which a selection commission is dissolved.

94.　　In the normal course of events the commission would be dissolved when the Lord Chancellor notifies a selection made by the commission. That is to say, when a selection of a person by the commission is accepted by the Lord Chancellor and the Lord Chancellor notifies the Prime Minister for recommendation of that person for appointment, the commission is dissolved, being functus officio (paragraph 10).

95.　　Paragraphs 11 – 12 provide that the commission will also be dissolved in various circumstances in which it ceases to be properly constituted. These are: if a member of the commission dies or becomes incapacitated; if a person nominated from a territorial commission either resigns his membership of the selection commission or ceases to be a member of the territorial commission from which he has been appointed; if someone who is a member of the commission by virtue of holding high judicial office ceases to hold that office; or if the non-legally qualified member (or members) of the commission ceases (or all cease) to be non-legally qualified.

96.　　Paragraphs 11(2) and 12(2) provide that in such cases, rather than the commission continuing with fewer members, or a changed balance of backgrounds, or a different balance of representation, a new selection commission has to be convened by the Lord Chancellor as soon as practicable after dissolution.

Part 3 Duty to Convene Commission: Special Rules

97. This part of the Schedule modifies the Lord Chancellor's duty to convene a selection commission under certain circumstances.

Selection commission for the office of Deputy President

98. Paragraph 13 provides that the duty on the Lord Chancellor to convene a selection commission for the office of Deputy President or for the office of Judge does not apply if a selection commission for the office of President has been convened or the Lord Chancellor is under a duty to convene such a selection commission. This means that if there is a vacancy or impending vacancy for the office of President this must be filled before any vacancy in the office of Deputy President which might arise at the same time. This "fill the senior office first" approach, which maximises the likelihood that there will be a President to chair commissions for other vacancies, is carried through for other vacancies by paragraph 14.

Selection commission for the Office of Judge

99. Paragraph 14 provides that the duty on the Lord Chancellor to convene a selection commission for the office of Judge does not apply if a selection commission for the office of President or Deputy President has been convened or the Lord Chancellor is under a duty to convene such a selection commission. This means that if there is a vacancy or impending vacancy for the office of President or Deputy President these must be filled before any vacancy for the office of Judge which might arise at the same time.

100. Paragraphs 13(2) and 14(2) state that the Lord Chancellor must convene a selection commission for the unfilled vacancies (in the office of Deputy President or Judge) as soon as practicable after the Lord Chancellor has selected a candidate put forward by the selection commission for the office of President or Deputy President.

Section 27: Selection process

101. This section sets out the overall process which must be undertaken by the selection commission (the composition of which is provided for in Schedule 8) before it makes a selection of one name (subsection 10) and puts this to the Lord Chancellor (under section 28). Subsection (1) sets out the duties of the commission with regard to the particular selection process to be applied to each vacancy under consideration.

102. As provided for in subsections (5) and (6) selection must be made solely on merit. The task of setting out the criteria or competences against which merit will be tested lies with the commission. The commission can only recommend those who meet the eligibility requirements set out in section 25. Under subsection (7) anyone who is a member of the commission cannot be selected (hence the provisions in Schedule 8 for identifying persons who wish to be considered for a particular vacancy and disqualifying them from membership of the commission).

103. Subsection (8) provides that the commission must, when making selections for the appointment of judges, also take into account the need for the Court to have among its judges those with knowledge and experience of practice in the law in every part of the United Kingdom. This is intended to maintain the convention that currently applies to the House of Lords that there should generally be at least 2 Scottish judges and usually 1 from Northern Ireland. The Lord Chancellor, as provided for by subsection (9), may issue non-binding

guidance to the commission about the vacancy that has arisen, for example on the jurisdictional requirements of the Court, which the commission must have regard to.

104.   Subsections (2) and (3) list the persons the commission must consult during the selection process (although it may consult others). They are (subsection (2)): senior judges (as defined by Section 60) who are neither on the commission nor willing to be considered for selection, the Lord Chancellor, the First Minister in Scotland, the Assembly First Secretary in Wales and the Secretary of State for Northern Ireland. In addition (subsection (3)), the commission must, if all the "senior judges" for a part of the United Kingdom are not able to be consulted (because they are candidates or members of the commission), consult the next most senior judge in that part who is able to be consulted. This ensures that there will always be some senior judicial input from every part of the United Kingdom into every selection process.

Section 28: Report

105.   This section sets out the stage after the commission has made a selection under the process set out in Section 27.

106.   Subsection (1) provides that after a selection has been made the commission must submit a report to the Lord Chancellor stating who has been selected and containing the information set out in subsections (2), (3) and (4) (that information being essentially that which is required to enable the Lord Chancellor to exercise his options under section 29 on a properly informed basis).

107.   Before choosing to exercise one of his options set out in section 29 the Lord Chancellor, having received the report, must (under subsection (5)) consult the senior judges (or other judges) who were consulted by the commission, the First Minister in Scotland, the Assembly First Secretary in Wales and the Secretary of State for Northern Ireland.

Section 29: The Lord Chancellor's options

108.   This section sets out the Lord Chancellor's options after he has received a name from the commission and carried out further consultation under section 28. It works in conjunction with section 30 which sets out the grounds on which the Lord Chancellor can exercise two of his options – to reject the selection commission's recommendation or to ask the selection commission to reconsider its recommendation. It outlines the three possible stages of the process and the options the Lord Chancellor has at those stages.

109.   Subsection (1) outlines the three possible stages. The first stage is where a person has been selected under section 27. The second stage is where a person has been selected following a rejection or reconsideration at stage 1. The third and final stage is where a person has been selected following a rejection or reconsideration at stage 2.

110.   Subsection (2) provides the Lord Chancellor with his options in dealing with stage 1 of the process. He may (a) notify the selection (which is to say, notify the Prime Minister of the selection for the Prime Minister to recommend that person to Her Majesty for appointment), (b) reject the selection or (c) require the commission to reconsider the selection. Should the Lord Chancellor exercise options (b) or (c) the process enters stage 2.

111.   Subsection (3) provides that during the second stage the Lord Chancellor can (a) notify the selection to the Prime Minister (as above), having exercised either option b) or c) in stage 1; (b) reject the selection if it was made following reconsideration at the first stage;

or (c) require the commission to reconsider the selection, but only if it was made following a rejection at stage 1. Should the Lord Chancellor exercise option (b) or (c) the process enters stage 3.

112.   At the third stage, as provided for in subsection (4), the Lord Chancellor must notify the selection although, as provided for in subsection (5), he may notify a candidate who was reconsidered at stage one or two but not rejected.

113.   The Lord Chancellor's options as set out in this section can be summarised as follows: He can:

      a) accept the recommendation;

      b) ask the commission to reconsider; or

      c) reject the recommendation.

114.   If the Lord Chancellor selects option b) first, he would ask the selection commission to reconsider. After reconsideration the commission, under section 31, can still put forward the same name with further reasons or recommend an alternative. The Lord Chancellor can then put forward either of the recommended candidates (unless he chooses to reject the second candidate put forward).

115.   Under option c) the Lord Chancellor can reject the name provided by the selection commission.

116.   If rejection follows reconsideration, under section 31 the selection commission must submit an alternative candidate. At this point the Lord Chancellor can either:

      a) accept this candidate; or

      b) accept the candidate originally put forward before reconsideration.

117.   If the Lord Chancellor rejects the original name provided by the selection commission, under section 31 it must submit an alternative candidate giving reasons for their choice. At this point the Lord Chancellor can either:

      a) accept the second candidate; or

      b) ask the selection commission to reconsider – The selection commission, under section 31, can then either resubmit the second candidate or an alternative candidate. If an alternative candidate is put forward the Lord Chancellor can then choose between the first name following rejection or the new name following reconsideration.

Section 30: Exercise of powers to reject or require reconsideration

118.   This section details the grounds upon which the Lord Chancellor can exercise his powers to reject or require reconsideration of a selection, as provided for in section 29.

119.   The right of rejection is only exercisable according to subsection (1) when in the Lord Chancellor's opinion the person selected is not suitable for the office concerned.

120.   The right to require reconsideration, as stated in subsection (2), is exercisable under three conditions subject to the Lord Chancellor's opinion. The Lord Chancellor can ask for reconsideration if he feels there is not enough evidence that the person is suitable for office; if

he feels there is not enough evidence that person is the best candidate on merit; or if there is not enough evidence that the judges of the Court will between them have enough knowledge of, and experience in the laws of each parts of the United Kingdom, following the new appointment.

121.   Should the Lord Chancellor exercise either of these options, under subsection (3) the Lord Chancellor must provide his reasons in writing.

Section 31: Selection following rejection or requirement to reconsider

122.   This section makes provision for the process that the selection commission must follow if the Lord Chancellor requests reconsideration of a selection, or rejects a selection, under section 29.

123.   As provided by subsections (2) and (3) the commission can never put forward a candidate whose selection has been rejected at any stage of the process.

124.   Subsection (3) provides that the commission can reselect a candidate whose selection the Lord Chancellor has requested be reconsidered or provide another candidate, but not a candidate whose selection has already been rejected.

125.   Subsection (4) states that the commission must inform the Lord Chancellor of the person selected following rejection or requirement for reconsideration.

Terms of Appointment

Section 32: Oath of allegiance and judicial oath

126.   This section provides for every judge of the Supreme Court (which includes the President and Deputy President) to be required to take the oath of allegiance to the Sovereign and the Judicial Oath, as soon as may be after accepting that office. The required oaths are described in subsection (6) and are set out in the Promissory Oaths Act 1868. Separate provision is made for the taking of the oaths on appointment as President, Deputy President, and judge.

127.   Subsection (1) requires the President to take the oaths in the presence of the Deputy President, or, if there is no Deputy President, the senior ordinary judge ("senior ordinary judge" being defined in section 60(3)(b)).

128.   Subsection (2) requires the Deputy President to take the oaths in the presence of the President, or, if there is no President, the senior ordinary judge.

129.   Subsection (3) provides that a judge of the Court (excluding the President and Deputy President – see subsection (5)) must take the oaths in the presence of the President, or, if there is no President, the Deputy President, or if there is no Deputy President, the senior ordinary judge.

130.   Subsection (4) provides that the President and Deputy President are required to take the oaths in terms of subsections (1) and (2) whether or not the person appointed as President or Deputy President has previously taken the oaths after accepting another office. For example, a person appointed as President having previously served as Deputy President will be required to take the oaths on appointment as President even though he took them on appointment as Deputy President.

131.   Subsection (5) provides that a judge of the Court who becomes a Supreme Court judge by virtue of his appointment directly to the Court as President or Deputy President does not have to take the oaths twice, by virtue of subsection (1) or (2) and of subsection (3) – that is to say, in those circumstances, the person appointed as President or Deputy President takes the oaths only once, on account of the appointment as President.

Section 33: Tenure

132.   This section provides for the judges of the Supreme Court to hold office while they are of good behaviour, as is presently the case for Lords of Appeal in Ordinary. This is of course subject to the possibility of resignation, and the provision for retirement, set out in sections 35 and 36. (This provision does not apply to persons who, under section 38 of the Act, are acting judges of the Supreme Court. See section 38(5)(b).)

133.   This section also provides, consistently with the position of all senior judicial office holders, that removal from office of any judge of the Supreme Court may only be effected following resolutions passed by both the House of Commons and the House of Lords.

Section 34: Salaries and allowances

134.   This section provides for judges of the Supreme Court to receive a salary and allowance, detailing how the salary and allowance is to be determined and from where the salary and allowance is paid. It is in terms which reproduce the effect of the provisions governing these matters for Lords of Appeal in Ordinary.

135.   Subsection (1) states that a judge of the Supreme Court is entitled to a salary, and subsection (2) that the amount of the salary is to be determined by the Lord Chancellor with the agreement of the Treasury. Subsection (3) makes transitional provision to the effect that at the commencement of the provisions establishing the Supreme Court, the salaries of the first judges of the Supreme Court will remain the same as those received by them as Lords of Appeal in Ordinary immediately before commencement. Subsection (4) provides for these salaries, consistently with other judicial salaries, to be capable of being increased but not reduced.

136.   Subsection (5) provides that the salary will be charged on and paid out of the Consolidated Fund of the United Kingdom.

137.   Subsection (6) provides that the Lord Chancellor may determine, in agreement with the Treasury, an allowance to be paid to a judge of the Court, which will be paid out of money provided Parliament. This is in addition to the judicial salary, to provide flexibility.

Section 35: Resignation and retirement

138.   This section makes provision for the resignation or retirement of judges of the Supreme Court.

139.   Under subsection (1) any judge of the Supreme Court (including the President and Deputy President) may at any time resign from that office. Resignation is effected by giving notice in writing to the Lord Chancellor.

140.   Subsection (2) makes separate provision for resignation from the office of President or Deputy President. The holder may so resign without resigning from the office of a judge of the Supreme Court. The resignation is again effected by giving notice in writing to the Lord Chancellor.

141.   Subsection (3) amends section 26(4)(a) of, and Schedule 5 to, the Judicial Pensions and Retirement Act 1993 (retirement), so that references to "Judge of the Supreme Court" will be substituted for "Lord of Appeal in Ordinary". The effect of this amendment is that the retirement age and associated provisions as to retirement which apply to Lords of Appeal in Ordinary will apply in the same way to judges of the Supreme Court.

Section 36: Medical Retirement

142.   This section makes provision analogous to that for other senior judicial office holders for vacation of the office of a judge of the Supreme Court (including the President and Deputy President) on medical grounds.

143.   Subsection (1) provides for the scope of the section: it applies if the Lord Chancellor is satisfied by means of a medical certificate that the person holding office as a judge of the Supreme Court is both disabled by permanent infirmity from performing his duties and for the time being is incapacitated from resigning from his office.

144.   In such circumstances, subsection (2) enables the Lord Chancellor to declare the office of the person in question to be vacated (subject to the conditions in subsection (4)). Subsection (3) provides for this declaration to have effect as though the person in question had himself or herself resigned on the date of the declaration. Subsection (4) requires the Lord Chancellor, before making a declaration, to secure the agreement of the appropriate judges of the Supreme Court (depending on the office which would be vacated). Without that agreement, the declaration will have no effect. In the case of an ordinary judge (as defined in section 60(3)(a)), the agreement required is that of the President and Deputy President of the Court; in the case of the President, the agreement required is that of the Deputy President and the senior ordinary judge (as defined in section 60(3)(b)); and in the case of the Deputy President, the agreement required is that of the President and the senior ordinary judge.

Section 37: Pensions

145.   Subsections (1) and (2) make amendments to the Judicial Pensions Act 1981 and Judicial Pensions and Retirements Act 1993 respectively, to substitute 'Judge of the Supreme Court' for 'Lord of Appeal in Ordinary'. These amendments are to ensure that the pension provision currently enjoyed by the Lords of Appeal in Ordinary will transfer over to the Justices of the Supreme Court, and that individual members of the Supreme Court who were previously Lords of Appeal in Ordinary will retain the pension benefits accrued in the former capacity and that those benefits will continue to accrue in the same way relative to their service as judges of the Supreme Court as they did relative to their service as Lords of Appeal in Ordinary.

146.   Furthermore, subsection (3) provides that the amendments made to the 1981 and 1993 Acts do not affect the operation of any provision or anything done under a provision in relation to the office of, or service as, Lord of Appeal in Ordinary. This ensures that any retired Lords of Appeal in Ordinary are not affected adversely by the changes to legislation.

Acting Judges

Section 38: Acting Judges

147.   This section makes provision enabling the Supreme Court to have access to additional Judges beyond its permanent membership to supplement the permanent members of the Supreme Court where necessary; sets out the mechanism for determining the "pool" from

which acting judges will be drawn; and sets out the terms and conditions of any service as an acting judge.

148.   Subsection (1) sets out the basic proposition that certain persons may act as judges of the Court if the President so requests. The persons who may be so requested are those who presently hold office as "senior territorial judges" (defined in subsection (8)), and those who are members of the supplementary panel (about which provision is made in section 39). As provided for in subsection (2) the Deputy President can make such a request if circumstances require.

149.   Subsection (3) amends the Judicial Pensions and Retirement Act 1993 with the effect that acting judges cannot sit in the Supreme Court after the age of 75, bringing them into line with the provisions for continued sitting by retired Lords of Appeal in Ordinary and other "Lords of Appeal" (other than the Lord Chancellor) entitled to sit in the House of Lords at present.

150.   Subsection (4) provides that any acting judge sitting in the Supreme Court should be treated for all purposes as a permanent judge of the Supreme Court (with the exception of the provisions as to appointment, tenure, remuneration, etc. listed in subsections (5) and (6)), and may accordingly perform any of the functions of a permanent judge of the Court.

151.   Subsection (7) provides for the remuneration and allowances for acting judges, which are to be determined by the Lord Chancellor with the agreement of the Treasury and paid from money provided by Parliament.

152.   Subsection (8) defines "senior territorial judge", as judges of the Court of Appeal in England and Wales and their counterparts at senior appellate level in Scotland and Northern Ireland.

Section 39: Supplementary panel

153.   This section makes provision for the constitution of the Court's supplementary panel (from which judges can be drawn to supplement the permanent membership of the Court).

154.   Subsection (1) provides that there is to be a supplementary panel, and subsections (2) and (3) make provision for its membership on commencement – in effect the same persons, with the exception of the Lord Chancellor and the Lords of Appeal in Ordinary (who will have become the judges of the Supreme Court), who are presently "Lords of Appeal" and able, by virtue of section 5(3) of the Appellate Jurisdiction Act 1876, to sit in proceedings in the Appellate Committee.

155.   After commencement, by virtue of subsection (4), a person will become a member of the supplementary panel on ceasing to hold office as a judge of the Supreme Court or as a senior territorial judge, provided approval is given as laid out in sub-paragraphs (a) and (b). There is a special rule if the person in question is the President of the Court (subsection (5)). In this case, by virtue of subsection (6), that person automatically becomes a member of the supplementary panel, unless he or she notifies unwillingness to become a member of the panel, was removed from office for misbehaviour, or retired from office on grounds of incapacity, as set out in paragraphs (a)-(c). Subsection (7), for the avoidance of doubt, makes it clear that ceasing to hold office as a senior territorial judge in order to take up office as a judge of the Supreme Court (and vice versa) does not trigger membership of the supplementary panel.

156.   Subsection (8) provides for resignation from the panel (by notice in writing to the President). Subsection (9) provides for retirement from the panel, which is to be at the age of 75 or five years after joining the panel, whichever is earlier. Subsection (10) provides that "senior territorial judge" has the same meaning as in section 38(8), and defines the term "qualifying judicial office" as being the office held by a person prior to becoming a member of the supplementary panel and on account of the holding of which that person was entitled to become a member of the panel.

Jurisdiction, relation to other courts etc

Section 40: Jurisdiction

157.   This section makes provision for the jurisdiction of the Supreme Court, which is in essence that of the House of Lords in appellate matters together with the jurisdiction of the Judicial Committee of the Privy Council in relation to devolution issues under the Scotland Act 1998, Government of Wales Act 1998 and Northern Ireland Act 1998.

158.   Subsection (1) provides that the Supreme Court is to be, as is the House of Lords, a superior court of record, and accordingly has the inherent powers of such a court.

159.   Subsections (2) and (3) reproduce the effect of section 3 of the Appellate Jurisdiction Act 1876, conferring on the Supreme Court the appellate jurisdiction exercised by virtue of that section by the House of Lords. The other appellate jurisdiction of the House of Lords, and the jurisdiction of the Judicial Committee of the Privy Council in relation to devolution issues, are transferred to the Supreme Court by virtue of subsection (4) and Schedule 9 (which is introduced by that subsection).

160.   Since the provisions work by transferring the existing jurisdiction, the appeal process (except to the extent that it would be covered by Supreme Court Rules made under section 45) and the types of appeal from each jurisdiction, including leave requirements, and the routes of recourse otherwise, will remain the same as is currently the case for the House of Lords and Judicial Committee of the Privy Council.

161.   Subsection (5) makes provision for the Supreme Court to have the power, as does the House of Lords, to determine any questions it deems necessary to determine, for the purposes of doing justice in an appeal to it, under this Act or any other Act.

Section 41: Relation to other courts etc

162.   This section makes provision as to the effect of decisions of the Supreme Court as judicial precedents. The essence of the provision is that a decision made by the Supreme Court under particular jurisdiction should have the same effect as a decision of the body in which the jurisdiction is currently vested (whether that is the House of Lords or the Judicial Committee of the Privy Council). So in the case of jurisdiction transferred from the House of Lords, a decision of the Supreme Court on an appeal from one jurisdiction within the United Kingdom will not have effect as a binding precedent in any other such jurisdiction, or in a subsequent appeal before the Supreme Court from another such jurisdiction. In the case of the devolution jurisdiction transferred from the Judicial Committee of the Privy Council, a decision of the Supreme Court will be binding in all legal proceedings except for subsequent proceedings before the Supreme Court itself.

163.   Subsection (1) provides that nothing in the provisions of the Act about the Supreme Court is to affect the distinctions between the separate legal systems of the parts of the United

Kingdom. This recognises that those legal systems are separate, and that there is a variety of distinctions between them, so that, for example, Scotland differs from Northern Ireland in some ways, and in other ways from England and Wales.

164.   Subsection (2) provides that a decision of the Supreme Court on an appeal from a court in one part of the United Kingdom is to be regarded as the decision of a court of that part of the United Kingdom. So, for example, a decision on appeal from the Court of Session would be regarded as a decision of a Scottish court, and would have binding effect in Scottish courts accordingly, but would not have binding effect in English courts (although it might, like the decision of the House of Lords in Donoghue v. Stevenson, be found by English courts to be so persuasive an authority as to be readily followed). Subsection (2) does not apply in relation to decisions in devolution proceedings.

165.   Subsections (3) and (4) make provision to maintain the status quo in relation to the effect of decisions in devolution proceedings.   The status quo is that, by virtue of section 103(1) of the Scotland Act 1998, section 82(1) of the Northern Ireland Act 1998 and paragraph 32 of Schedule 8 to the Government of Wales Act 1998, a decision of the Judicial Committee of the Privy Council in the exercise of its devolution jurisdiction is "binding in all legal proceedings (other than proceedings before the Committee)".

166.   Subsection (3) accordingly provides that a decision of the Supreme Court on a devolution matter will not bind the Court itself when subsequently making a decision on a devolution matter, but will otherwise be "binding in all legal proceedings", mirroring the wording of section 103(1) of the Scotland Act 1998 and its counterparts.

167.   Subsection (4) defines "devolution matter", by reference not only to those matters which are "devolution issues" in the Scotland Act, Northern Ireland Act and Government of Wales Act, but also to the possibility of a reference to the Court, under the Scotland Act and Northern Ireland Act alone, of the question whether a Bill or part of a Bill of the Scottish Parliament or Northern Ireland Assembly is within the Parliament's or Assembly's legislative competence.

Composition for Proceedings

168.   The Supreme Court will, like the House of Lords, be able to sit in panels. Section 42, together with section 43, makes provision for the composition of panels. The underlying rule is that no panel should ever consist wholly or predominantly of non-permanent judges, but that otherwise, the Court should have considerable flexibility (essentially mirroring that of the Appellate Committee), including the flexibility, subject to the agreement of the parties, to commence or continue hearing proceedings notwithstanding that a judge is unable to continue.

Section 42: Composition

169.   Subsections (1), (2) and (3) provide for the basic rule that an uneven number of judges equal to or greater than three must be designated to hear any proceedings - there is no flexibility to designate an even number of judges. Given that an uneven number must be designated, permanent judges have to be in the majority in order to ensure that the composition is never wholly or predominantly of non-permanent judges (subsection (1)(c)).

170.   This does not mean that the actual hearing cannot commence before an even number of judges, as the judges will by definition have been designated to hear proceedings in

advance of the beginning of the hearing proper, and section 42 is, as subsection (4) makes clear, subject to section 43, which allows for additional flexibility. Subsection (5) makes it clear that the power to require more than three judges to be designated for particular proceedings or a particular class or classes of proceedings is exercisable by the President of the Court; and subsection (6) makes provision which ensures that the sections work on the basis that the Court is constituted for proceedings when the judges are designated to hear those proceedings (rather than when the hearing commences).

Section 43: Changes in Composition

171.   This section provides for flexibility in the event of the Court being reduced in number (for example due to death or illness) before the end of proceedings.

172.   Subsection (1) provides for this section to apply if the Court ceases to be duly constituted "because one or more members of the Court are unable to continue". In such a case, subject to any directions which the President may give (subsection (4)), the presiding judge (defined in subsection (6) as the judge who is to preside over the proceedings, or is presiding if they have already commenced) may direct that the Court is still duly constituted (subsection (2)), but only if the parties agree, the Court still consists of at least three judges, and at least half of those judges are permanent judges. So the Court may continue with an even number of judges; and if it does, and the judges divide evenly in their decisions, the case must (subsection (5)) be re-argued before a Court constituted in accordance with section 42 .

173.   Because the section applies (by virtue of section 42(6)) to any proceedings from the time that judges are designated to hear proceedings (rather than when the proceedings commence), the Court is (for example) enabled to start the hearing with four judges where five were designated but one is unable to continue, as long as at least two of the four are permanent judges. The provision in subsection (1), that the section applies to a court constituted in accordance with a direction 'under this section', is to allow for the possibility of two judges falling out of a panel which started off with at least five. This might occur if, for example, a panel of five is designated, and before the hearing commences, one judge is unable to continue, and the presiding judge directs (the parties being in agreement and there still being four judges of whom at least two are permanent) that the Court is still duly constituted; and then another judge is unable to continue, leaving three, of whom two are permanent, and the parties are still in agreement that the proceedings should continue. Then there would be a Court which ceases to be duly constituted "in accordance with this section", but the presiding judge may direct that it is still duly constituted.

Practice and Procedure

Section 44: Specially qualified advisers

174.   This section makes provision for the Supreme Court to have specially qualified advisers to assist it in its work for the purpose of hearings that may require specialist support. This derives from existing provision in the Supreme Court of Judicature Act 1891 (section 3) and the Judicial Standing Orders of the House of Lords (Order XVI).

175.   Subsection (1) makes the basic provision empowering the Court, if it thinks it is necessary, to hear and dispose of proceedings, either wholly or in part, with the assistance of one or more specially qualified advisers.

176.   Subsection (2) provides that any remuneration payable to an expert adviser is to be determined by the Court unless otherwise agreed between the adviser and the parties to the proceedings. This remuneration, as set out in subsection (3), will form part of the costs of the proceedings.

Section 45: Making of Rules

177.   This section, together with section 46, sets out how Rules of Court will be made for the Supreme Court.

178.   Subsection (1) provides for the President of the Supreme Court to make rules dealing with the Court's practice and procedure. This power is in part analogous to the way in which the House of Lords regulates its work through its Standing Orders and Practice Directions.

179.   Subsection (2) provides that the power to make rules includes the power to provide rules for different cases, including different proceedings such as civil and criminal proceedings and on devolution matters.

180.   Under subsection (3) the President is obliged to exercise the rule-making power with a view to ensuring that the Court is accessible, fair and efficient and the rules are simple and simply expressed.

181.   Subsection (4) places a duty on the President, before making Supreme Court Rules, to consult the Lord Chancellor, the principal legal professional bodies of the different parts of the United Kingdom (listed in subsection (5)), and such other bodies, representing persons likely to be affected by the Rules, as the President considers it appropriate to consult.

Section 46: Procedure after Rules made

182.   By virtue of subsection (1), Rules made by the President are to be submitted to the Lord Chancellor, and by virtue of subsection (2), Rules so allowed are to come into force on such day as the Lord Chancellor directs, and be contained in a statutory instrument to which the Statutory Instruments Act 1946 will apply as if it contained rules made by a Minister of the Crown. Such an instrument is, by virtue of subsection (3), to be subject to negative resolution procedure.

Section 47: Photography etc

183.   This section removes the prohibition on photography in section 41 of the Criminal Justice Act 1925 and in section 29 of the Criminal Justice Act (Northern Ireland) 1945 (both of which prohibit the taking of photographs in all courts) in relation to the Supreme Court, by changing the definition of 'court' in those provisions to include all courts of justice except the Supreme Court.

Staff and resources

184.   Sections 48 to 51 together make provision for the resourcing and funding arrangements for the Supreme Court.   They establish the post of Chief Executive of the Supreme Court within a clear statutory framework, which places certain duties on the Chief Executive and the Lord Chancellor. The Chief Executive will be responsible for the non-judicial functions of the Court and anything delegated to him by the President under section 50 (in effect allowing the Chief Executive to be formally responsible for appointing staff to the Court).   In doing so the Chief Executive will be answerable to the President, in accordance with whose directions he will be required to act in carrying out his functions

(although not so as to override any other duty or restriction on his powers). The Chief Executive will be responsible for ensuring that the Court's resources are used to provide an efficient and effective system to support the Court in carrying on its business. The Lord Chancellor has a corresponding duty under section 50 to provide accommodation for the Court and to provide other resources to allow the Chief Executive to carry out his responsibilities. The resourcing arrangements will operate as follows:

- The administrative service for the Supreme Court will be headed by a Chief Executive, a civil servant appointed by a process involving an *ad hoc* commission.

- The staff of the Court will be civil servants, accountable to the Chief Executive and not to the Lord Chancellor.

- The Chief Executive will be principally answerable to, and operating under the day-to-day guidance of, the President of the Court.

- The President of the Supreme Court and the Chief Executive will determine the bid for resources for the Court in line with Governmental spending review timescales.

- The bid will be passed to the Lord Chancellor, who will include it as a separate line in the overall DCA bid submitted to the Treasury.

- The Lord Chancellor will be responsible for directly dealing with the Treasury to secure resources for the Court during the Spending Review process.

- The Treasury will scrutinise the overall DCA bid and approve the overall financial expenditure for the DCA group in the Spending Review period including the Supreme Court.

- Following the settlement DCA will give a separate Departmental Expenditure Limit (DEL) to the UK Supreme Court.

- The Chief Executive of the Supreme Court will submit an estimate to HM Treasury which will then be presented before the House of Commons as part of the overall estimates.

- The House of Commons will approve the overall estimates and transfer resources accordingly.

- Because the Supreme Court will have its own estimate, the funds approved will be transferred to the Court direct from the Consolidated Fund, not via the DCA.

- The Chief Executive will be the Accounting Officer for the Supreme Court and so directly accountable to the Court and to Parliament, rather than being subject to the DCA Permanent Secretary as Principal Accounting Officer.

Section 48: Chief Executive

185. Subsection (1) establishes the office of Chief Executive, to be appointed under subsection (2) by the Lord Chancellor after consulting the President of the Court. In accordance with subsection (3) the Chief Executive will be responsible for all the non-judicial functions of the Court and any function of appointing officers and staff under section 49(1) that is delegated to him by the President of the Supreme Court. The President is expected to delegate all his functions under section 49(1), so this means that in effect the

Chief Executive will appoint staff for the Supreme Court. Under subsection (4), the Chief Executive will carry out his functions in accordance with any directions given by the President.

Section 49: Officers and Staff

186. Subsection (1) makes provision for the President of the Supreme Court to have formal responsibility for appointing staff to the Supreme Court. This function may be delegated to the Chief Executive. Under subsection (2) the Chief Executive will be able to determine the staffing needs and arrangements in agreement with the Lord Chancellor and in accordance with the Court's overall budget. Subsections (3) and (4) provide that, as both the staff of the Court and the Chief Executive will be civil servants, the civil service pension arrangements will apply accordingly.

Section 50: Accommodation and Other Resources

187. Under subsection (1) the Lord Chancellor is responsible for ensuring that the Supreme Court is provided with such accommodation as he thinks appropriate for the Court to carry on its business. The Lord Chancellor is also responsible for providing such other resources as he thinks appropriate for the Court to carry on its business. This complements section 48, which sets out the duties of the Chief Executive. The Chief Executive will not be able to carry out his duties if the Lord Chancellor does not provide appropriate resources.

188. Subsection (2) provides that the Lord Chancellor can discharge his general duty under subsection (1) by directly providing accommodation or other resources or by entering into arrangements with third parties for their provision; and subsection (3) makes available for this purpose certain powers to acquire land for public service.

189. This section additionally, under subsection (4), enables the Scottish Ministers to make a contribution towards the resource running costs of the Court. This contribution (which will be related to the proportion of the costs of civil business attributable to appeals from Scotland) will be made by a transfer of resources from an appropriate budget.

Section 51: System to support Court in carrying on business

190. Subsection (1) places the Chief Executive under the duty to ensure that the resources provided under the preceding section are used to provide an efficient and effective system to support the Court in carrying on its business. The Chief Executive is therefore responsible for the effective administration of the Court. Subsection (2) makes provision for the key responsibilities of the Chief Executive in undertaking his general duty under subsection (1).

Fees

Section 52: Fees

191. This section should be read together with section 53, which makes supplementary provision about fees. Section 52(1) provides for the Lord Chancellor to have a power, by order (which by virtue of section 144 is to be exercisable by statutory instrument subject to negative resolution procedure) to prescribe the fees payable in respect of any matter dealt with by the Supreme Court. By virtue of subsection (2), this includes a power to exempt, remit or reduce fees, and to specify the criteria by which exemptions, reductions and remissions are to operate. The exercise of the power to prescribe fees is, by virtue of

subsection (3), subject to a duty on the Lord Chancellor to have regard to the principle that access to the courts should not be denied.

192.   By virtue of subsections (4)-(6), the exercise of the power is also subject to a requirement of prior consultation with the President and Deputy President of the new Supreme Court and the senior judiciary in each of the three jurisdictions of the United Kingdom, and the principal legal professional bodies in those jurisdictions.

Section 53: Fees: Supplementary

193.   This section supplements section 52. Subsection (1) provides that Supreme Court fees are to be recoverable as a civil debt (mirroring the general position in relation to court fees).

194.   Subsection (2) places the Lord Chancellor under a duty to take such steps as are reasonably practicable to bring information about fees to the attention of those who are likely to have to pay them.

195.   Subsection (3) defines "Supreme Court fees" (as fees prescribed in an order under section 52).

Annual report

Section 54: Annual Report

196.   Subsection (1) places a duty on the Chief Executive of the Supreme Court to prepare a report as soon as practicable after the end of each financial year (defined in subsection (3)) about the business of the Supreme Court, and to send it to the Lord Chancellor and to the heads of the three devolved administrations. By virtue of subsection (2), the Lord Chancellor is required to lay that Report before both Houses of Parliament.

Supplementary

Section 55: Seal

197.   This section makes provision for the Supreme Court to have an official seal, and for that seal to be judicially recognised so as not to require further proof of documents emanating from the Court.

Section 56: Records of the Supreme Court

198.   This section amends the Public Records Act 1958 to ensure that records of the Supreme Court are included among the "court records" under the general supervision of the Public Records Office. This is achieved by amending the list in paragraph 4(1) of Schedule 1 to the Public Records Act 1958 to add to the list of courts therein an entry for the Supreme Court.

199.   In addition this section makes provision for the Chief Executive of the Supreme Court to have custody of the records of the Court by virtue of his office as chief executive, rather than by virtue of a determination by the Lord Chancellor to this effect.

Section 57 and Schedule 10: Proceedings under jurisdiction transferred to Supreme Court

200.   Section 57 introduces Schedule 10, which makes transitional provision relating to proceedings which, at the time the Supreme Court is established, are pending in the House of

Lords or Judicial Committee of the Privy Council under jurisdiction which is transferred to the Supreme Court. The essence of the approach is that such proceedings may be continued in the Supreme Court after the transfer of the jurisdiction as if they had commenced in the Supreme Court, and anything done in accordance with the rules applicable to proceedings in the House of Lords or Judicial Committee (as the case may be) is to be treated as having been done in accordance with the corresponding rules of the Supreme Court. In addition, there is a saving for any acts, decisions or orders of the House of Lords or Judicial Committee in proceedings under a transferred jurisdiction, which will have the same effect, with further proceedings pursuant to or in respect of them being possible, as if they were acts, decisions or orders of the Supreme Court.

Section 58: Northern Ireland Act 1998: excepted and reserved matters relating to the Supreme Court

201. This section relates to the status of the UK Supreme Court under the Northern Ireland Act 1998. It provides that the Supreme Court is to be an excepted matter but that rights of appeal to the Supreme Court and legal aid for such appeals are to be reserved matters. In so doing it ensures that the position of the UK Supreme Court reflects the current status of the judicial function of the House of Lords.

Section 59: Renaming of Supreme Courts for England and Wales and Northern Ireland

202. This section makes provision for the renaming of the Supreme Court of England and Wales and the Supreme Court of Judicature of Northern Ireland.

203. Subsection (1) provides that the Supreme Court of England and Wales is renamed the Senior Courts of England and Wales. Subsections (2) and (3) provide respectively that the Supreme Court of Judicature of Northern Ireland is renamed the Court of Judicature of Northern Ireland and that the Northern Ireland Supreme Court Rules Committee is renamed the Northern Ireland Court of Judicature Rules Committee.

204. Subsection (4) provides for references to those bodies in other legislation and in any "instrument or other document" (so as to cover, for example, court forms) to have effect as references to those bodies as renamed.

205. Subsection (5) introduces Schedule 11, which provides additionally for direct textual amendment of numerous references in other legislation to one or other of the existing Supreme Courts.

Schedule 11: Renaming of Supreme Courts for England and Wales and Northern Ireland

206. Schedule 11 works in conjunction with section 59 to give effect to the renaming of the Supreme Court of England and Wales and the Supreme Court of Judicature of Northern Ireland. Schedule 11 provides for direct textual amendments of the numerous references in other legislation to one or other of the existing Supreme Courts.

207. Part 1 re-titles the Supreme Court Act 1981, Supreme Court (Offices) Act 1997, the Rules of the Supreme Court (Northern Ireland) 1980 and the Rules of the Supreme Court (Northern Ireland) (Revision) 1980, and provides for references to those enactments wherever they occur in any other enactment to be changed to references to those enactments as retitled.

208.   Part 2 covers the vast majority of the legislation which refers to the Supreme Court of England and Wales: paragraph 4 lists legislation in which the only references needing amendment are simply to "the Supreme Court", and provides for all those references to be changed to references to "the Senior Courts".

209.   Part 3 corresponds to Part 2: Paragraph 5 provides for references to a person being required to be a solicitor of the Supreme Court of Northern Ireland (which constitute the majority of references in UK legislation to the Supreme Court of Northern Ireland) to be replaced by references to a solicitor of the Court of Judicature; and paragraph 6 covers, in the same way as paragraph 4, legislation which refers to the Supreme Court of Northern Ireland.

210.   Part 4 deals with references in other legislation which require more tailored amendment. Of particular importance are the amendments made to the Interpretation Act 1978 by paragraph 18 of the Schedule. The definition of "Supreme Court" in Schedule 1 to the 1978 Act is amended so that "Supreme Court" is defined as the Supreme Court of the United Kingdom and will have that meaning wherever it appears in the statute book unless a contrary intention appears. In addition, the existing entries defining "Supreme Court" are replaced by entries defining "Senior Courts" and "Court of Judicature" respectively.

Section 60: Interpretation of Part 3

211.   Subsection (1) defines 'part of the United Kingdom', 'the senior judges' and 'the Supreme Court' for the purposes of Part 3 of the Act.

212.   Subsection (2) defines the term 'high judicial office' for the purposes of Part 3 of the Act. This expression is used in the requirements of eligibility for qualification as a Supreme Court judge in section 25, and in the requirements of eligibility to serve as an acting judge under sections 38 and 39. This definition replaces that in section 25 of the Appellate Jurisdiction Act 1876.

213.   Subsection (3) defines the terms 'ordinary judge' and 'senior ordinary judge' (which are of particular importance in determining the person before whom oaths are to be taken on appointment, and who will chair and sit on the selection commission provided for in Schedule 8, should the President and Deputy President be unable to sit). An "ordinary judge" is defined in subsection (3)(a) as a judge of the Supreme Court other than the President or Deputy President. The "senior ordinary judge" is defined in subsection (3)(b) as the ordinary judge who has served longest as a judge of the Court (whether over one or more periods and whether or nor always as an ordinary judge). Subsection (4) "carries over" seniority for this purpose, providing that service as a Lord of Appeal in Ordinary counts as service as judge of the Court in defining the senior ordinary judge.

PART 4: JUDICIAL APPOINTMENTS AND DISCIPLINE

SUMMARY

214.   Chapter 1 of Part 4 creates a Judicial Appointments Commission (which is subject to more detailed provisions in Schedule 12), and a Judicial Appointments and Conduct Ombudsman (which is subject to more detailed provisions in Schedule 13). Chapter 2 sets out the process to be followed by the Commission and by the Lord Chancellor in appointing the Lord Chief Justice and other Heads of Division, the Lords Justices of Appeal, and puisne High Court judges and other judicial office holders. Chapter 2 also provides for complaints about the appointments process to be made to the Judicial Appointments and Conduct

Ombudsman. Chapter 3 makes provision for a disciplinary procedure in relation to the judiciary, applicable when the Lord Chancellor is considering whether to exercise his statutory powers to remove a judicial office-holder, with the concurrence of the Lord Chief Justice; and when the Lord Chief Justice is considering whether to impose any lesser disciplinary sanction on such an office-holder, with the concurrence of the Lord Chancellor. There are new powers enabling the Lord Chief Justice to advise, warn or formally reprimand judicial office holders as a result of the disciplinary process, to suspend them in certain circumstances, subject to the agreement of the Lord Chancellor, and to make regulations and rules about the process, with the agreement of the Lord Chancellor. Chapter 3 also allows complaints to be made to the Judicial Appointments and Conduct Ombudsman about judicial disciplinary cases. Chapter 4 makes provision about interpretation.

BACKGROUND

215.   The selection and appointment of judges in England and Wales has been primarily the responsibility of the Lord Chancellor. In carrying out this function, he is supported by officials from the Department for Constitutional Affairs. The precise responsibility for the actual appointments themselves varies according to the type of judicial appointment:

- Appointments to the offices of Lord of Appeal in Ordinary, the Heads of Division of the Supreme Court (retitled the Senior Courts by the Act) and Lord Justice of Appeal are made by The Queen on the recommendation of the Prime Minister as the Sovereign's principal adviser. It has been the practice that the Prime Minister seeks advice from the Lord Chancellor in the first instance.

- Appointment to the offices of High Court Judge, Circuit Judge, Recorder, District Judge (Magistrates' Courts), Social Security Commissioners, the Judge Advocate General and the Judge Advocate of Her Majesty's Fleet are made by The Queen on the recommendation of the Lord Chancellor.

- The Lord Chancellor bears personal responsibility for making a wide range of full-time and part-time appointments to the judiciary, including to the offices of District Judge (Civil) and Deputy District Judge, and to a wide range of tribunals, including certain tribunals with a UK-wide jurisdiction.

216.   The administration of the judicial appointments system is carried out on the Lord Chancellor's behalf by staff of the Legal and Judicial Services Group in the Department for Constitutional Affairs. A principal function of the Group is to supply all the information and advice which the Lord Chancellor requires to enable him to fulfil his responsibilities in this field, and to provide him with the material on which to make a fair and informed judgement about every appointment. This includes corresponding with and informing and interviewing those who are, or may become, candidates for appointment; consulting judges, members of the profession and others as required; administering the selection procedures; following and executing the Lord Chancellor's instructions and guidance, both on individual appointments and candidates; providing feedback as required on individual applications and on his general policy.

217.   The Act creates a new independent Judicial Appointments Commission, which will assume responsibility for the process of selecting people for judicial appointments in England and Wales and for those appointments to UK-wide tribunals made by the Lord Chancellor. The Judicial Appointments Commission will select one candidate for each vacancy and report

that selection to the Lord Chancellor. Schedule 14 to the Act lists the offices below the High Court for which the Commission will make selections, and no one may be appointed to such office who has not been selected by the Commission. The Lord Chancellor will either appoint or recommend for appointment the selected candidate, or will have the ability to reject a candidate, once, and to ask the Commission to reconsider, once. Having exhausted these options, the Lord Chancellor must appoint or recommend for appointment whichever candidate is selected. The Act makes special provision for the appointment of the Lord Chief Justice and Heads of Division and of Lords Justices of Appeal; in these cases the Commission will establish a selection panel of four members, consisting of two senior judges (normally including the Lord Chief Justice) and two lay members of the Commission. The appointments of Lords Justices and above will continue to be made by The Queen formally on the advice of the Prime Minister after the Commission has made a recommendation to the Lord Chancellor.

218. Schedule 12 sets out the membership of the Judicial Appointments Commission, and its powers and responsibilities, which will reflect its status as an Executive Non-Departmental Public Body. There will be a lay Chairman and five other lay members, five judicial members, two legal professionals, a tribunal member and a lay magistrate. They will be supported by a Chief Executive and staff. The Act requires that selections for judicial appointment shall be made solely on merit. In addition, the Commission has a statutory duty to have regard to the need to encourage diversity in the range of persons available for selection. The Lord Chancellor will be able to issue guidance to the Commission, which they must have regard to, but the detailed appointments procedures they will follow are a matter for them, and not prescribed in the Act. Guidance can only be issued after consultation with the Lord Chief Justice and after being approved in draft by both Houses of Parliament.

219. The Lord Chancellor has statutory powers to remove judicial office holders below the High Court (including tribunal members and lay magistrates) from office for incapacity or misbehaviour. These powers are amended by Schedule 4 so that they can be exercised only with the agreement of the Lord Chief Justice (or in the case of certain UK tribunal members who sit mainly in Scotland or Northern Ireland, with the agreement of the Lord President of the Court of Session or the Lord Chief Justice of Northern Ireland as appropriate). The Lord Chancellor has also had a more general disciplinary power in relation to judicial office holders, and has considered complaints about judicial conduct, and where necessary has advised, warned or formally reprimanded office holders. Part 4 of the Act makes statutory provision for a disciplinary system in relation to judicial office holders, in cases falling short of removal, in which the Lord Chief Justice will have the power to advise, warn or reprimand judicial office holders following disciplinary proceedings, with the agreement of the Lord Chancellor. These provisions will apply to judicial office holders in England and Wales and to those members of UK-wide tribunals who are appointed after selection by the Judicial Appointments Commission. There is also provision in section 118 for the disciplinary provisions to be extended to other office holders who are removable by the Lord Chancellor. Section 108 makes it clear that these provisions do not affect the Lord Chief Justice's general ability to speak informally to any judge on any matter which concerns him without having to inform or obtain the agreement of the Lord Chancellor. The Lord Chief Justice will also be given a new statutory power to suspend judges from sitting in certain circumstances, with the agreement of the Lord Chancellor. The Lord Chief Justice will also have the power to make regulations and rules governing disciplinary cases, with the agreement of the Lord

Chancellor, and subject to Parliamentary scrutiny in the case of regulations. The Judicial Appointments and Conduct Ombudsman will be able to consider complaints about disciplinary cases.

220.   It will remain the case that judges of the High Court and above can be removed only by The Queen on an Address from both Houses of Parliament.

COMMENTARY ON SECTIONS

Chapter 1: Commission and Ombudsman

Section 61: The Judicial Appointments Commission

221.   Section 61 establishes a Judicial Appointments Commission. Schedule 12 makes further provision about the Commission itself. The appointments below the High Court in which the Commission will be involved are listed in Schedule 14.

Schedule 12: The Judicial Appointments Commission

Part 1 The Commissioners

222.   This part of Schedule 12 sets out the size and balance of membership of the Judicial Appointments Commission.

Paragraphs 1-6 The Commissioners

223.   Paragraph 1 requires there to be a chairman and 14 other Commissioners, to be appointed by The Queen on the recommendation of the Lord Chancellor.

224.   Paragraph 2 provides for the chairman to be a lay member. Of the other Commissioners, 5 must be judicial members, 2 must be professional members, 5 must be lay members, 1 other must be the holder of an office listed in Part 3 of Schedule 12 (which lists members of tribunals and other similar office holders who will be appointed by the Lord Chancellor), and 1 other must be a lay justice member. The judicial members must be made up of one Lord Justice of Appeal, one puisne judge of the High Court, one judge who is either a Lord Justice of Appeal or a puisne judge of the High Court, one Circuit Judge and one District Judge or a person appointed to an office under section 89 of the Supreme Court Act 1981 (i.e. the offices of Senior Master of the Queen's Bench Division, Chief Chancery Master, Chief Taxing Master, Chief Bankruptcy Registrar and Senior District Judge of the Family Division). The two professional members must be a practising barrister and a practising solicitor. A Commissioner only counts towards the total in the category to which he was appointed, so that a lay member, for example, does not become a professional member if he qualifies as a practitioner.

225.   Paragraph 3 specifies that a person cannot be appointed as a Commissioner if he is a civil servant. This is to ensure that the Commission is not subject to any covert or improper Governmental influence.

226.   Paragraph 4 details what is meant by judicial, professional, lay and lay justice member. A judicial member holds one of the offices specified in paragraph 2(3) (set out above) and is not a practising lawyer (defined in paragraph 6 as a practising solicitor or barrister in England and Wales, a solicitor or advocate in Scotland and a Solicitor or member of the Bar in Northern Ireland which includes those employed to give legal advice or providing legal advice under a contract for services). A professional member is a barrister or

solicitor practising in England and Wales (again further defined in paragraph 6 to include employed lawyers and those who give legal advice under a contract for services). A lay member is an England and Wales resident who has never been a holder of a listed judicial office (by paragraph 6, an office listed in Schedule 14) or a practising lawyer.

227.   Paragraph 5 allows the Lord Chancellor to increase the size of the Commission, by increasing the size of any or all of the different categories of Commissioner. He can do this by order, but only with the agreement of the Lord Chief Justice, and subject to affirmative resolution in both Houses of Parliament (by virtue of section 144(5)(e) of this Act). This is to prevent a Lord Chancellor seeking improperly to influence selections by altering the balance of the Commission in one direction or another at his own unchecked discretion.

228.   Paragraph 6 provides definitions of terms used in the Schedule.

Paragraph 7 Selection of Commissioners

229.   Paragraph 7 provides that in appointing the three senior judicial members of the Commission (the judges drawn from the Court of Appeal and the High Court) the Lord Chancellor may recommend to Her Majesty only people selected by the Judges' Council, which must give reasons for its selection. The Judges' Council is defined as the body designated for that purpose by the Lord Chief Justice. Other Commissioners will be appointed after being selected by a panel convened by the Lord Chancellor. Paragraph 7(2) provides the Lord Chancellor may only recommend people as the other 12 Commissioners if he has appointed a panel for the purposes of selection of Commissioners and they have been selected by that panel. Provision about the composition of the panel is made in paragraph 8.

Paragraph 8 Panels

230.   Paragraph 8 provides for a panel to select the Commissioners, with the exception of the three senior Judges. The panel will comprise four members, unless the appointment being made is that of the chairman of the Judicial Appointments Commission, when there will be no fourth member. The first member (who will be the chairman of the panel) is chosen by the Lord Chancellor with the agreement of the Lord Chief Justice (or if the post of Lord Chief Justice is vacant then with the agreement of the senior Head of Division). The second member will be the Lord Chief Justice or his nominee, unless the office of the Lord Chief Justice is vacant, when it will be the senior Head of Division or his nominee. The third member will be chosen by the chairman. The fourth member will be the chairman of the Judicial Appointments Commission, when there is one and that is not the post being appointed to. Members of the panel must not be civil servants. In addition the chairman of the panel must not be a Commissioner, a member of the Commission's staff, a practising lawyer, a judicial office holder listed in Schedule 14, or a member of the House of Commons. The third member must not be a member of the House of Commons. In selecting the first member, consideration must be given as to whether the person being appointed has previously exercised any judicial functions or has any past service as a civil servant, a Commissioner, a member of the Commission's staff, a practising lawyer, a judicial office holder listed in Schedule 14, or any past or present political activity or affiliations which would make them inappropriate for appointment. The first member must apply the same considerations in nominating the third member. These provisions are intended to ensure the neutrality of the panel, including its political neutrality.

231.   Paragraph 9 provides for the Lord Chancellor to pay the panel fees and expenses.

Paragraph 10 Selection by a panel

232.   The panel must take account of any views expressed by the Bar Council and Law Society in appointing the barrister and solicitor members respectively. Before selecting the chairman and the other lay members, the panel must consider the same questions that apply in selecting the first and third members of the panel, in relation to whether they have exercised any functions or have any political affiliations which make them inappropriate for the appointment. Those functions are expressed in broadly the same terms as for the first member as set out above, but also include past employment in the civil service. In selecting lay members, the panel must seek to ensure, as far as practicable, that one of the selected lay members has special knowledge of Wales.

Paragraph 11 Vice-chairman

233.   This paragraph provides that the senior judicial member of the Commission will be the vice-chairman. The vice-chairman will be able to exercise the functions of the chairman, other than those of sitting on the panel for selecting members of the Commission and sitting on the selection panels for Heads of Division and for Lords Justices of Appeal, for which, in the absence of the chairman, a lay Commissioner is required.

Paragraphs 12- 15 Term of office etc. of Commissioners

234.   Paragraphs 12 to 15 provide for the term of office of the Commissioners. They will serve for two fixed terms of up to five years, meaning that their maximum period of service is 10 years. Commissioners cease to be Commissioners if they cease to qualify for the category of membership under which they were appointed. However, the Lord Chancellor may allow Commissioners to continue in office for a specified period even if they have ceased to fall within the category to which they were appointed. For example, if a member had particular skills or a background which was required for a particular competition that was being run by the Commission, then the Lord Chancellor might allow him to continue in office until the competition was over. Commissioners also lose office if they are appointed to the civil service, but they may not be continued in office where this is the case. If a Commissioner resigns he must do so in writing to The Queen. Commissioners can be removed from office by The Queen on the recommendation of the Lord Chancellor. Paragraph 15 (2) specifies the conditions in which the Lord Chancellor may recommend that a Commissioner be removed from office. They are that the person has failed to exercise their functions for a continuous period of six months; or they have been convicted of an offence; or they have been made bankrupt; or are otherwise unfit to hold office or unable to exercise its functions.

Paragraph 16 Salary, allowances and expenses

235.   This paragraph makes provision for the Commission to pay fees, expenses, pensions and any other allowances in respect of Commissioners and former Commissioners. These payments will be determined by the Lord Chancellor.

Paragraph 17 Code of conduct

236.   This paragraph provides for the Lord Chancellor to issue and revise a code of conduct to be observed by the Commissioners.

Part 2 The Commission

237.   Part 2 sets out the status and functions of the Commission.

Paragraph 18 Status of the Commission and its property

238.   This paragraph specifies that the Commission is not to be regarded as part of the Crown or, therefore, of the Government; it will be a non-departmental public body.

Paragraph 19 Powers

239.   This paragraph allows the Commission to do anything to enable it to perform its functions, but does not allow the Commission to borrow money unless the Lord Chancellor has given permission for it to do so.

Paragraph 20 Committees

240.   This paragraph allows the Commission to establish committees, and its committees to establish sub-committees, in order for it to undertake its business, and allows activities to be delegated by the Commission to a committee and by a committee to a sub-committee. Only Commissioners may be members of the committees and sub-committees. Committees or sub-committees charged with making selections for judicial appointments must include at least one judicial and one lay member. The Commission will of course be advised by its staff, and by anyone else invited to give advice, and it may rely on interviewing panels made up of non-Commissioners, but final decisions are the responsibility of the Commissioners. The requirements of this paragraph in relation to committees and sub-committees do not apply to the selection panels for senior appointments, which are provided for separately in sections 71 and 80 of the Act.

Paragraph 21 Procedure and proceedings

241.   This paragraph specifies that the Commission may control how it conducts its business and those of its committees and sub-committees including the numbers of members that must be present to make the proceedings valid, which in the case of a committee or sub-committee exercising functions of selection set out in Part 4 of the Act must be 3. The proceedings of the Commission or a committee or a sub-committee are still valid even if one of the posts on the Commission is unoccupied or if the appointment of a member is defective.

Paragraph 22 Staff

242.   This paragraph makes provision requiring the Commission to appoint a Chief Executive and allowing it to appoint staff (which may include staff who transfer from other Government departments) to enable it to undertake its objectives. The Lord Chancellor has to agree the appointment of the Chief Executive. The terms and conditions of service with the Commission will be set by the Commission and agreed by the Lord Chancellor. The Commission will pay staff, as set out in their terms and conditions and in doing so will take account of the pay and terms and conditions operating in the Civil Service. The Commission is added to Schedule 1 to the Superannuation Act 1972. The Commission must pay for any increase attributable to its inclusion in the Schedule to the Superannuation Act 1972 that the Minister of the Civil Service requires. Staff of the Commission are not servants or agents of the Crown, neither do they have the Crown's status, immunity or privileges.

Paragraph 23 Arrangements for assistance

243.   This paragraph allows for the Commission, with the agreement of the Lord Chancellor, to make arrangements for people to provide assistance to it. This would enable it to contract out services as it sees fit and in doing so to pay for such services.

Paragraphs 24 and 25 Appointments and arrangements by the Lord Chancellor

244. This paragraph allows the Lord Chancellor to appoint a Chief Executive for an interim period prior to a Chief Executive being appointed in accordance with paragraph 23(1)(a). The Chief Executive appointed by the Lord Chancellor may undertake matters on behalf of the Commission including incurring expenditure, appointing staff and making arrangements for people to provide assistance to the Commission subject to any directions given by the Lord Chancellor.

245. Paragraph 25 allows the Lord Chancellor to appoint staff to the Commission and to make contracting out arrangements as appropriate. The Lord Chancellor cannot exercise these powers after the end of 3 years from the date on which the Commission is first constituted under paragraph 1, or at such earlier time as the Commission itself may decide. If a Chief Executive has been appointed to the Commission, the Lord Chancellor cannot exercise these powers without the Chief Executive's agreement.

Paragraph 26 Power to transfer staff to employment of the Commission

246. This paragraph makes provision for the Lord Chancellor to make regulations for relevant staff to be transferred to the Commission. Such staff must be current civil servants who are providing assistance in the Commission. Before making these regulations the Lord Chancellor must consult organisations that appear to him to represent the interests of those likely to be affected by the regulations, such as trade unions. The Lord Chancellor can only exercise this power before the Commission is first constituted in accordance with paragraph 1 and, with the agreement of the Commission, during the period of 3 years from that time.

Paragraph 27 Delegation

247. This paragraph provides for the Commission, a committee or sub-committee or the Chief Executive to delegate any activities to staff, secondees, and to people providing assistance e.g. those with whom contracting out arrangements are made or who are providing services in connection with such arrangements. The Commission, a committee or a sub-committee cannot delegate its function of making selections in relation to judicial appointments.

Paragraph 28 Delegation and contracting out of superannuation functions

248. This paragraph allows powers in relation to the Superannuation Act 1972 to be delegated to the Chief Executive and then allows such powers to be delegated by the Chief Executive to anyone he authorises. The Chief Executive or his delegate may authorise the contracting out of any superannuation functions but the Commission or the Chief Executive may revoke such an authorisation at any time.

Paragraph 29 Inspection of documents

249. This paragraph requires the Commission to allow anyone authorised by the Lord Chancellor, for example auditors, to look at or to copy accounts and any other papers which the Lord Chancellor considers relate to the Commission's expenditure. In doing this, the Commission must give such explanations of the material as the Lord Chancellor may require.

Paragraph 30 Financial provisions and directions

250. This paragraph provides for the Lord Chancellor to pay the amount of money to the Commission that he determines to be appropriate for it to exercise its functions. It also allows

the Lord Chancellor to require the Commission not to incur specific or total expenditure above a specified threshold without the consent of the Lord Chancellor and to follow specified procedures in relation to its costs and expenditure, to ensure he has the appropriate financial control over the Commission, for which he will be ultimately accountable to Parliament.

Paragraph 31 Accounts and audit

251.   This paragraph obliges the Commission to maintain proper financial systems and to prepare accounts each financial year, which are an accurate reflection of its income and expenditure. In preparing its accounts, which must be sent to the Lord Chancellor when he directs, the Commission must comply with any instructions from the Lord Chancellor and the Treasury. The accounts must be sent to the Comptroller and Auditor General on or before 31 August for the financial year last ended, who will scrutinise them and prepare a report which, together with the accounts, will be laid before each House of Parliament.

Paragraph 32 Reports

252.   This paragraph specifies that the Commission will produce annually for the Lord Chancellor a report detailing its activities. The Lord Chancellor, after consulting the Lord Chief Justice, may oblige the Commission to deal with any particular subject in all or any of its annual reports. In addition, the Lord Chancellor may require the Commission to report at any time on any matter he directs. The annual report must be laid before Parliament and published. Other reports which, for example, might contain confidential information, would not be laid before Parliament.

Paragraphs 33 - 35 Documentary evidence

253.   These paragraphs allow for a Commissioner or an authorised member of the Commission's staff to sign under the Seal of the Commission to authorise documentary evidence. Contracts and instruments need not be under the Seal if entered into by properly authorised individuals designated for a general or specific purpose. A document that is under the Seal of the Commission or signed on behalf of the Commission is to be received in evidence and is to be taken to be duly authorised unless the contrary is proved.

Paragraph 36 General

254.   This paragraph specifies that the Commission's first financial year begins when the Commission is established and ends the following 31 March. Subsequent financial years run from 1 April to 31 March. Commissioners are disqualified from election to the House of Commons by inserting a reference to the Judicial Appointments Commission into Part 2 of Schedule 1 to the House of Commons Disqualification Act 1975. The Commission is included in the list of public authorities for the purposes of the Freedom of Information Act 2000 by inserting a reference to the Commission into Part 6 of Schedule 1 to that Act.

Section 62: The Judicial Appointments and Conduct Ombudsman

255.   Section 62 establishes a Judicial Appointments and Conduct Ombudsman. Provisions about this office appear in sections 99 to 105, sections 110 to 114 and in Schedule 13.

Schedule 13: The Judicial Appointments and Conduct Ombudsman

256.   Schedule 13 provides for the constitution and procedure of the Judicial Appointments and Conduct Ombudsman.

Paragraphs 1 and 2 The Ombudsman

257.   These paragraphs provide for the Ombudsman to be appointed by The Queen on the recommendation of the Lord Chancellor. A person may not be appointed if he is a civil servant or if he has ever been a practising lawyer (defined in paragraph 2 in the same terms as the definitions in Schedule 12) or a holder of a judicial office listed in Schedule 14. Before recommending a person the Lord Chancellor must also consider whether the person has exercised functions of a judicial nature, or has been a member of the Judicial Appointments Commission, member of staff of the Commission, member of the House of Commons, a civil servant or whether any present or past political activity or affiliations would make the person inappropriate for the appointment.

Paragraphs 3-5 Term of office etc. of Ombudsman

258.   These paragraphs provide that the Ombudsman will be appointed for a fixed period of no more than 5 years in the first instance. He may serve for no more than ten years in all. There are provisions for his resignation or removal from office, and grounds for the latter are set out. They are that the Ombudsman has ceased to meet the conditions for appointment set out above or has ceased to be appropriate for appointment because of the considerations set out above, has failed to exercise their functions for a continuous period of six months; or that he has been convicted of an offence; or that he has been made bankrupt; or that he is otherwise unfit to hold office or unable to discharge its functions.

Paragraph 6 Salary, allowances and expenses

259.   This paragraph provides for the Ombudsman's remuneration and pension, and for the possibility of the payment of compensation in special circumstances on his ceasing to hold office.

Paragraph 7 Acting Ombudsman

260.   This paragraph allows for the appointment of an acting Ombudsman in the circumstances set out in sub-paragraph 7(1). These are if the office becomes vacant, if the Lord Chancellor considers that the Ombudsman is unable to exercise his functions or if there is a conflict of interest in relation to a particular matter. The person so appointed would have to be eligible for appointment as Ombudsman. The paragraph also provides for the payment and pension of the acting Ombudsman and for the circumstances in which his appointment may come to an end, for instance because the situation that gave rise to him being needed has ended.

Paragraph 8 Status of the Ombudsman

261.   This paragraph provides that the Ombudsman is to be a corporation sole.

Paragraph 9 Powers of the Ombudsman

262.   Paragraph 9 allows the Ombudsman to do anything to enable him to perform his functions, but does not allow him to borrow money or acquire real property, or to appoint staff other than in accordance with paragraph 10.

Paragraph 10 Arrangements for assistance

263.   Paragraph 10 allows the Ombudsman, with the agreement of the Lord Chancellor, to make arrangements for assistance to be provided to him. This would include contracting out

services as it sees fit and in doing so to pay for such services. It is intended that the Ombudsman will be supported by civil servants seconded to his office, as happens with the Parliamentary Commissioner.

Paragraph 11 Arrangements by the Lord Chancellor

264.   Paragraph 11 allows the Lord Chancellor to make such arrangements for assistance for the Ombudsman if the latter has not done so.

Paragraph 12 Delegation of functions

265.   Paragraph 12 allows the Ombudsman to delegate his functions, but requires him to sign any report or recommendation.

Paragraph 13 Financial provisions and directions

266.   Paragraph 13 provides for the Ombudsman's expenses to be met by the Lord Chancellor, and for the latter to be able to issue him with directions on the procedures to be used in relation to his costs and expenditure, and on limits in relation to expenditure, or any particular type of expenditure, above which the Lord Chancellor's prior approval must be obtained.

Paragraph 14 Code of conduct

267.   As with the Commissioners, the Lord Chancellor may issue a code of conduct to be observed by the Ombudsman.

Paragraph 15 Reports

268.   Paragraph 15 provides that the Ombudsman must produce an annual report which must be laid before Parliament and published. The Lord Chancellor may direct him to deal with a particular matter in either that report or an ad hoc one. There is no statutory requirement for an ad hoc report to be laid before Parliament or published.

Paragraph 16 Documentary evidence

269.   Paragraph 16 provides that a document signed by or on behalf of the Ombudsman is to be received in evidence, unless proved to be inauthentic.

Paragraph 17 General

270.   Paragraph 17 specifies what is meant by financial year, the first of which will begin when the Commission is established and end the following 31 March. The Ombudsman will be barred from election to the House of Commons by inserting a reference to the post into Part 3 of Schedule 1 to the House of Commons Disqualification Act 1975; and the Ombudsman will be listed as a public authority for the purposes of the Freedom of Information Act 2000 by inserting a reference to the post into Part 6 of Schedule 1 to that Act.

Chapter 2: Appointments

General Provisions

Section 63: Merit and good character

271.   Section 63 requires that selections by the Commission (or a selection panel, in relation to senior appointments) must be solely on merit, and that the selecting body must be satisfied that the person selected is of good character.

Section 64: Encouragement of diversity

272.   Section 64 requires the Commission to have regard to the need to encourage diversity in the range of people available for selection, subject to the duty to select solely on merit and the duty to select a person of good character.

Section 65: Guidance about procedures

273.   Section 65 provides a power for the Lord Chancellor to issue guidance to the Commission or a selection panel about the exercise, firstly, of its function of identifying persons willing to be considered for selection and, secondly, of its function of assessing them. The purposes for which guidance may be given include the encouragement of diversity in the range of persons available for selection. The Commission and any selection panel under it must have regard to such guidance. Guidance cannot overrule the statutory requirements that selections be made solely on merit, and that those selected be of good character. The procedure for issuing the guidance is set out in section 66.

Section 66: Guidance: supplementary

274.   Section 66 provides that before issuing any guidance under section 65 the Lord Chancellor must consult the Lord Chief Justice and lay a draft of the proposed guidance before Parliament. The draft guidance will be subject to the affirmative resolution procedure. Guidance may be revised and reissued from time to time, in which case the same procedures must be complied with. Guidance may also be revoked by order; such an order is subject to the negative resolution procedure by virtue of section 144(6). The Lord Chancellor must consult the Lord Chief Justice before revoking any guidance.

Lord Chief Justice and Heads of Division

Section 67: Selection of Lord Chief Justice and Heads of Division

275.   Section 67 provides that recommendations to The Queen to appoint candidates to the senior judicial posts of the Lord Chief Justice and the Heads of Division (the Master of the Rolls, President of the Queen's Bench Division, President of the Family Division and Chancellor of the High Court) can only be made in accordance with the procedures set out in the Act.

Section 68: Duty to fill vacancies

276.   Section 68 imposes a duty on the Lord Chancellor to fill any vacancies in the offices of Lord Chief Justice or the Heads of Division.   But, for as long as the Lord Chief Justice agrees, he may leave a vacancy in any of the offices of the Heads of Division unfilled.

Section 69: Request for selection

277. Section 69 provides for the Lord Chancellor to request the Commission to select someone for appointment as Lord Chief Justice or as one of the Heads of Division. Before making a request the Lord Chancellor must consult the Lord Chief Justice unless that post is vacant, or the holder of that post is incapacitated.

Section 70: Selection Process

278. Section 70 provides that on receiving a request to select a person for appointment as Lord Chief Justice or one of the Heads of Division, the Commission must appoint a selection panel, which will decide the process to be followed and make the selection of one person for each vacant post. The panel must consult the current holder of the relevant office, if that is practicable, and will be given administrative support by the Commission, of which it will be a committee. Selection panels for senior appointments are a special form of committee of the Commission.

Section 71: Selection Panel

279. The selection panel will have four members. The first member will be the most senior judge of the Supreme Court established by the Act who was a judge of England and Wales before being appointed to the Supreme Court and who is not disqualified, or another senior judge nominated by him. He will chair and will have a casting vote. The second member will be the Lord Chief Justice or his nominee, except where the Lord Chief Justice is disqualified or there is no Lord Chief Justice, in which case it will be another senior judge chosen by the most senior Supreme Court Judge. The third member will be the chairman of the Commission or his nominee, or if that post is vacant or the chairman is unavailable and has been unable to make a nomination, one of the lay members of the Commission chosen by themselves. The fourth member will be a lay member of the Commission chosen by the third member. A person is disqualified from being a member of the panel if that person is the current holder of the office being selected for, or if that person is willing to be considered for selection for that office.

Section 72: Report

280. After making its selection the panel must report to the Lord Chancellor, in a form approved by him, telling him who has been selected and providing him with any other information he requires. After submitting its report the panel must provide any further information the Lord Chancellor requires.

Section 73: The Lord Chancellor's options

281. When the Lord Chancellor receives the report informing him of the person selected by the panel, he has the options of accepting the selection; rejecting that person and requiring a different name to be put forward; or requiring the selection panel to reconsider its selection. This is stage 1 of the process. If the Lord Chancellor rejects the selection or requires reconsideration, the process moves into stage 2. At this stage the panel puts a name to the Lord Chancellor, and the Lord Chancellor has these options: he may accept the selection; he may reject the selection (but only if he has not already used that power at stage 1); or he may require reconsideration (but only if he has not already used that power at stage 1). If the Lord Chancellor rejects the selection or requires reconsideration, the process moves into stage 3. At this stage the panel again puts a name to the Lord Chancellor. This time he must accept

the selection of the latest selected candidate, or of a candidate selected in stage 1 or stage 2 whose name was not resubmitted by the panel after reconsideration, but who has not been rejected.

Section 74: Exercise of powers to reject or require reconsideration

282.   The Lord Chancellor can only reject a selection outright if, in his opinion, the person selected is not suitable for the office concerned. He can only require reconsideration if, in his opinion, there is not enough evidence that the selected person is suitable for the office concerned, or there is evidence that the person is not the best candidate on merit. If the Lord Chancellor either rejects a selection or requires it to be reconsidered, he must give his reasons in writing.

Section 75: Selection following rejection or requirement to reconsider

283.   If the Lord Chancellor rejects a candidate at stage 1 or stage 2, the panel must make a new selection, and may not reselect the rejected candidate, or reselect a candidate whose selection it previously withdrew after reconsideration. If the Lord Chancellor requires reconsideration at stage 1 or stage 2, the panel may confirm its selection, or may select a different person, but may not select a candidate who has already been rejected. The panel must inform the Lord Chancellor of its selection. These provisions do not prevent a rejected candidate, or one whose selection was withdrawn after reconsideration, from being selected for appointment on a subsequent occasion when the Lord Chancellor makes a request for a selection.

Lords Justices of Appeal

Section 76: Selection of Lords Justices of Appeal

284.   A similar process applies to the appointment of Lords Justices of Appeal. Section 76 provides that a person may only be recommended for appointment to one of these posts in accordance with the procedures in the Act.

Section 77: Duty to fill vacancies

285.   Section 77 imposes a duty on the Lord Chancellor to fill any vacancy in the office of Lord Justice of Appeal. The Lord Chancellor can only decide not to fill a vacancy whilst the Lord Chief Justice agrees that it may remain unfilled.

Section 78: Request for selection

286.   Section 78 provides for the Lord Chancellor to request the Commission to select someone for appointment as a Lord Justice of Appeal. Before asking the Commission to select someone the Lord Chancellor must consult the Lord Chief Justice. Any request may relate to more than one post and recommendation.

Section 79: Selection Process

287.   When the Lord Chancellor makes a request the Commission must appoint a selection panel, which will determine the procedure to be applied, apply the process and make a selection of one person for each vacancy. The panel is a committee of the Commission, which will provide it with administrative support.

Section 80: Selection Panel

288.   For the appointment of Lords Justices of Appeal, the selection panel will consist of four members. The first member is the Lord Chief Justice or another senior judge nominated by him, who will chair and have a casting vote; the second member is one of the Heads of Division or a Lord Justice chosen by the Lord Chief Justice; the third member is the Chairman of the Commission or his nominee, or if that post is vacant or the chairman is unavailable and has been unable to make a nomination, one of the lay members of the Commission chosen by themselves; and the fourth member is another lay member of the Commission chosen by the third member. No one who is willing to be considered for selection may be a member of the panel. No nominee may represent more than one person or be a member of the panel in another capacity.

Section 81: Report

289.   When the panel has selected someone, it must report to the Lord Chancellor, in a form approved by him, with the name of the person selected and any other information he requires. After submitting the report it must provide any further information the Lord Chancellor requires.

Section 82: The Lord Chancellor's options

290.   As in relation to the appointment of the Heads of Division, when the Lord Chancellor receives the report informing him of the person selected by the panel, he has the options of accepting the person selected; rejecting that person and requiring a different name to be put forward; or requiring the selection panel to reconsider its selection. This is stage 1 of the process. If the Lord Chancellor rejects the selection or requires reconsideration, the process moves into stage 2. At this stage the panel puts a name to the Lord Chancellor, and the Lord Chancellor has these options: he may accept the person selected; he may reject the selection (but only if he has not already used that power at stage 1); or he may require reconsideration (but only if he has not already used that power at stage 1). If the Lord Chancellor rejects the selection or requires reconsideration, the process moves into stage 3. At this stage the panel again puts a name to the Lord Chancellor. This time he must accept the selection of the latest selected candidate, or of a candidate selected in stage 1 or stage 2 whose name was not resubmitted by the panel after reconsideration, but who has not been rejected.

Section 83: Exercise of powers to reject or require reconsideration

291.   The Lord Chancellor can only reject a selection outright if, in his opinion, the person selected is not suitable for the office concerned. He can only require reconsideration if, in his opinion, there is not enough evidence that the selected person is suitable for the office concerned, or there is evidence that the person is not the best candidate on merit. If the Lord Chancellor either rejects a selection or requires it to be reconsidered, he must give his reasons in writing.

Section 84: Selection following rejection or requirement to reconsider

292.   If the Lord Chancellor rejects a selection, the panel cannot put forward the same candidate, or one whose selection has already been withdrawn after being reconsidered. If he requires reconsideration, the panel may reselect the same candidate, but not one who has already been rejected. In either case, the panel must inform the Lord Chancellor of its new or reconsidered selection. A person who has been reconsidered or rejected is not prevented

from being selected by the panel in response to a subsequent new request from the Lord Chancellor to select someone for appointment as a Lord Justice.

Puisne judges and other office holders

Section 85: Selection of puisne judges and other office holders

293.   Section 85 provides that sections 86 to 93 of the Act apply to a recommendation for the appointment by The Queen of a puisne judge of the High Court; a recommendation for the appointment by The Queen to any of the offices listed in Part 1 of Schedule 14; and an appointment by the Lord Chancellor to any of the offices listed in parts 2 and 3 of Schedule 14. The Lord Chancellor has a power to amend the Schedule by order in order to add or delete offices and references to statutes. Section 144 provides that any such order is subject to the negative resolution procedure in parliament, unless the order amends Part 1 of the Schedule 14 (which lists offices below the High Court to which The Queen makes appointments), in which case by section 144(5)(a) it is subject to affirmative resolution in both Houses.

Schedule 14: the Judicial Appointments Commission: relevant functions and offices

294.   Schedule 14 lists in Part 1 judicial and tribunal appointments below the High Court which are formally made by the Queen, with the relevant appointing powers; Part 2 lists judicial and other appointments made by the Lord Chancellor to posts whose holders will not be eligible to be appointed as a member of the Judicial Appointments Commission under Schedule 12 paragraph 2(2)(d); Part 3 lists appointments made by the Lord Chancellor to those tribunal and similar posts whose holders will be eligible to be appointed as a member of the Judicial Appointments Commission under Schedule 12 paragraph 2(2)(d). None of these appointments may be made unless the Commission has selected the person concerned.

Section 86: Duty to fill vacancies

295.   Section 86 imposes a duty on the Lord Chancellor to fill vacancies in the office of puisne judge of the High Court and the other offices listed in Parts 1, 2 and 3 of Schedule 14. But, whilst the Lord Chief Justice agrees, the Lord Chancellor can leave any such vacancy unfilled.

Section 87: Request for selection

296.   Section 87 enables the Lord Chancellor to request the Commission to select someone for appointment as a puisne judge of the High Court or to any of the offices listed in Schedule 14. Before asking the Commission to select someone the Lord Chancellor must consult the Lord Chief Justice.   Any request may relate to more than one recommendation or appointment. The Lord Chancellor is able to withdraw or modify requests in accordance with the provisions of section 95.

Section 88: Selection Process

297.   Section 88 requires the Commission to decide on and run a selection process and make a selection of one person for each post. In the course of doing so it must consult the Lord Chief Justice and another person who has held the office concerned or has relevant experience. If the selection process has not identified candidates of sufficient merit to be appointed, the Commission will not be able to make a selection, and section 88(2) and section 93 will apply.

Section 89: Report

298.   Section 89 provides that after it has run the selection process, the Commission must submit a report to the Lord Chancellor, in a form approved by him, which describes the process; names the person selected for each post, or states if it has not been able to make a selection; states any recommendations which the Lord Chief Justice and the other person with relevant experience made when they were consulted under section 88 and gives reasons if the Commission has not followed their recommendations; and contains any other information required by the Lord Chancellor. After submitting the report the Commission must provide any further information required by the Lord Chancellor.

Section 90: The Lord Chancellor's options

299.   In the same way as in relation to more senior appointments, when the Lord Chancellor receives the report informing him of the person selected by the Commission, he has three options. He can accept the selected person; reject that person and require a different name to be put forward; or require the Commission to reconsider its selection. This is stage 1 of the process. If the Lord Chancellor rejects the selection or requires reconsideration, the process moves into stage 2. At this stage the Commission puts a name to the Lord Chancellor, and the Lord Chancellor has these options: he may accept the selected person; he may reject the selection (but only if he has not already used that power at stage 1); or he may require reconsideration (but only if he has not already used that power at stage 1). If the Lord Chancellor rejects the selection or requires reconsideration, the process moves into stage 3. At this stage the Commission again puts a name to the Lord Chancellor. This time he must accept the selection of the latest selected candidate, or of a candidate selected in stage 1 or stage 2 whose name was not resubmitted by the Commission after reconsideration, but who has not been rejected.

Section 91: Exercise of powers to reject or require reconsideration

300.   The Lord Chancellor can only use his power in section 90 to reject a selection outright if, in his opinion, the person selected is not suitable for the office concerned, or for particular functions of that office. He can only require reconsideration if, in his opinion, there is not enough evidence that the selected person is suitable for the office concerned or for particular functions of that office, or there is evidence that the person is not the best candidate on merit. If the Lord Chancellor either rejects a selection or requires it to be reconsidered, he must give his reasons in writing.

Section 92: Selection following rejection or requirement to reconsider

301.   If the Lord Chancellor rejects a selection, the Commission must submit a new name it has not previously selected for the post. If the Lord Chancellor requires the Commission to reconsider, it may submit the same name, but not the name of someone who has already been selected and rejected. This does not prevent someone being selected in a subsequent appointments process. Having made its selection, the Commission must inform the Lord Chancellor.

Section 93: Reconsideration of decision not to select

302.   Section 88, which provides for the Commission to apply a selection process in response to a request from the Lord Chancellor, allows for the fact that the Commission may find that the selection process has not identified candidates of sufficient merit for them to

make a selection. Section 93 provides that if the Commission informs the Lord Chancellor that it is unable to make a selection because there are no candidates of sufficient merit, he may require it to reconsider, and they must inform him of any person then selected. If the Commission makes a selection on reconsideration, the Lord Chancellor will have the same options in relation to appointment as in ordinary cases.

Section 94: Duty to identify persons for future requests

303.   Section 94 enables the Commission to recruit in advance a pool of potential candidates for appointment to a particular class of posts. As requests to fill specific appointments of that class arise, they can then select people from that pool. . These people will not be guaranteed selection for actual appointments. The Lord Chancellor will initially give the Commission an indication of the numbers of people that are expected to be needed at a particular level and over a specific time. The Commission will identify suitable people taking into account the number of appointments that have been requested and report to the Lord Chancellor saying how far it has identified suitable people and provide any other information to assist the Lord Chancellor. As part of the process the Commission will be required to consult the Lord Chief Justice and someone with experience of the office concerned. If the Commission decides not to follow a recommendation made during the consultation process it must give reasons for not doing so in its report on the competition.

Section 95: Withdrawal and modification of requests

304.   Section 95 enables the Lord Chancellor to withdraw or modify a request under section 69, 78 or 87 of the Act in three particular circumstances. First, if the request was to fill a vacancy, he may only withdraw or modify the request with the agreement of the Lord Chief Justice (who has to agree to any decision not to fill an existing post). This situation could arise where there is a change in circumstances or simply because the predictions as to the number of vacancies likely to arise was wrong. Secondly, if the request was other than to fill a vacancy and would have resulted in the creation of additional posts, he may withdraw or modify such a request after consulting the Lord Chief Justice. Thirdly, if he considers that the process of identifying candidates by the Commission or the selection panel was not satisfactory or not applied satisfactorily, he may withdraw a request as a whole, after consulting the Lord Chief Justice, provided that he has not made any recommendations or appointments resulting from that request. The withdrawal or modification of a request (for whatever reason) must be by notice in writing from the Lord Chancellor to the Commission. The notice must state the circumstances and, if it relates to an unsatisfactory process, the reasons why the Lord Chancellor considers it to be so.

Section 96: Effect of acceptance of selection

305.   Section 96 allows the Commission to perform health checks on successful candidates for appointment, if the Lord Chancellor requires, and to report the results to the Lord Chancellor. If the checks are satisfactory the Lord Chancellor will appoint or recommend for appointment the person selected. If for any reason the Lord Chancellor rejects the candidate on health grounds he must consult the Lord Chief Justice. Selections can also be disregarded where the candidate does not accept an appointment when it is offered or is not available within a reasonable time to take up post.

Section 97: Scotland and Northern Ireland

306.   The Lord Chancellor has responsibility for appointing members of certain tribunals with a UK-wide jurisdiction, some of whose members sit wholly or mainly in Scotland or in Northern Ireland. Section 97 provides that, where consultation with the Lord Chief Justice is required under section 87(2), 88(3), 94(3), 95(2)(a), (b) or (c) or 96(4)(a), and where the consultation appears to relate to an appointment of a person that exercises functions wholly or mainly in Scotland or Northern Ireland, the Lord President of the Court of Session, or the Lord Chief Justice of Northern Ireland respectively will be consulted, rather than the Lord Chief Justice of England and Wales.

Assistance in connection with other appointments

Section 98: Assistance in connection with other appointments

307.   In addition to his responsibilities for senior judicial appointments in England and Wales and the other judicial appointments listed in Schedule 14, the Lord Chancellor has a role in identifying, nominating or recommending candidates for other judicial posts, including, for example, members of various international courts and tribunals. Many of these are ad hoc appointments, not judicial appointments in England and Wales. In some cases the appointments are not formally within the remit of the United Kingdom Government. It is therefore not possible for them to be listed in Schedule 14 and placed formally within the remit of the Judicial Appointments Commission. Section 98 therefore gives the Lord Chancellor the power to ask the Commission for assistance in such cases. This assistance may range from merely giving advice on how to proceed to running a selection process and selecting a candidate. Before requiring the Commission to give ad hoc assistance of this kind, the Lord Chancellor must consult the Lord Chief Justice and the Commission itself.

Complaints and references

Section 99 : Complaints: interpretation

308.   Section 99 describes two types of complaint about the appointment process: a Commission complaint, where the complaint is about the Commission's handling of a candidate for judicial appointment's application; and a departmental complaint, where the complaint is about the Lord Chancellor or his Department's handling of the application. Those entitled to complain are those who have applied for selection or have been selected, and claim to have been adversely affected by the maladministration about which they are complaining. It will not be possible under the Act for other members of the public to complain about the fact that someone else has, or has not, been selected for judicial appointment.

Section 100: Complaints to the Commission or the Lord Chancellor

309.   Section 100 requires the Commission and the Lord Chancellor to make arrangements for handling the complaints made to them. It will not, however, be mandatory for either of them to investigate a complaint that is made more than 28 days after the matter complained of. Complainants will need to make a complaint under this section before they can complain to the Ombudsman about maladministration in making an appointment.

Section 101: Complaints to the Ombudsman

310.   Section 101 provides that the Ombudsman must consider complaints which have been made under section 100 if the complainant refers the complaint to the Ombudsman within 28 days of the complainant being notified of the Commission or Lord Chancellor's decision in relation to their original complaint. If the Ombudsman does not think the complaint requires investigation he must inform the complainant; otherwise he must conduct an investigation. The Ombudsman has discretion to consider complaints received out of time. Any complaints made to the Ombudsman must be in a form approved by him. Section 101 goes on to provide that unresolved complaints made to the existing Commissioners for Judicial Appointments at the time these provisions are brought into force will be transferred to the Ombudsman, who will have a discretion to investigate them. No further complaints to the Commissioners for Judicial Appointments about such matters will be possible.

Section 102: Report and recommendations

311.   The Ombudsman must prepare a report on his findings on a complaint, with any recommendations, including any recommendation for the payment of compensation. Compensation would only be payable for loss suffered as a result of maladministration, and not in respect of any earnings the complainant would have received had his application for appointment been successful.

Section 103: Report procedure

312.   The Ombudsman must submit his report in draft to the Lord Chancellor, and to the Commission, if it was a Commission complaint. The Ombudsman must have regard to their proposals for amendment, and if their proposals are not reflected in his final report he must include a statement of those proposals. The Ombudsman must send the final report to the Lord Chancellor and, if it was a Commission complaint, to the Commission. He will also send a copy of the report to the complainant, but this version is not to contain confidential information relating to someone other than the complainant and the disclosure of which would otherwise be prohibited by section 139.

Section 104: References by the Lord Chancellor

313.   Section 104 allows the Lord Chancellor to refer to the Ombudsman any matters relating to the Commission's procedures, and for the Ombudsman to report on his investigations. The report, which must be signed by the Ombudsman personally, will include his findings and any action he recommends.

Section 105: Information

314.   The Commission and the Lord Chancellor must provide the Ombudsman with any information he reasonably requires relating to his investigations.

Miscellaneous

Section 106 : Consultation on appointment of lay justices

315.   Section 106 inserts a new subsection (2A) into Section 10 of the Courts Act 2003, which sets out the appointments process for lay justices. This provision provides that, in following the two stage process of appointment and assignment provided for in the Courts Act, the Lord Chancellor will be obliged to consult people who have special knowledge of

matters relevant to the appointment of a lay justice for a particular area. In practice, the Lord Chancellor is likely to meet this requirement by consulting the local Advisory Committee.

Section 107: Disclosure of information to Commission

316.   Section 107 allows the Commission to carry out confidential checks on applicants for judicial appointment. If an applicant is selected for appointment checks may be carried out with the police, the National Criminal Intelligence Service, the National Crime Squad and HM Revenue and Customs. The Lord Chancellor will also be able to designate by order under the negative resolution procedure other bodies with which confidential checks may be made. These are likely to include the Law Society in relation to solicitors, the Bar Council in relation to barristers, and the General Medical Council in relation to the appointment of medical practitioners to certain tribunals. The material that is required is for the purposes of deciding whether the applicant is suitable to hold judicial office.

Chapter 3: Discipline

Procedures

Section 108 : Disciplinary Powers

317.   Section 108 will form the basis of a disciplinary system in relation to senior judicial office holders in England and Wales and the holders of offices listed in Schedule 14. In accordance with the section the Lord Chancellor may only exercise his statutory powers to remove judicial office holders in accordance with prescribed procedures (which are defined by section 122 as procedures prescribed by the Lord Chief Justice with the agreement of the Lord Chancellor in regulations made under section 115 or rules made under section 117). Following the formal disciplinary process the Lord Chief Justice may formally advise or formally warn or reprimand, a judicial office holder, but only in accordance with prescribed procedures and with the agreement of the Lord Chancellor. As provided in subsection (3) this does not affect the ability of the Lord Chief Justice to speak informally to any judge about any matter of concern, or to issue general advice or warnings to the judiciary.

318.   The Lord Chief Justice may also, with the agreement of the Lord Chancellor, suspend a judicial office holder from exercising the functions of his office if the office holder is subject to criminal proceedings; is serving a sentence for a criminal offence; is subject to disciplinary proceedings following a conviction; or if, following a criminal conviction, it has been decided not to remove the judicial office holder from office, but the Lord Chief Justice and Lord Chancellor agree that a period of suspension is required in order to maintain confidence in the judiciary. Senior judges may be suspended during proceedings for an Address in Parliament to remove them from office. Office holders who are listed in Schedule 14 may be suspended during criminal or disciplinary investigations, prior to any conviction.

Section 109: Disciplinary powers: interpretation

319.   Section 109 defines for the purposes of section 108 when a judge is subject to criminal proceedings, or to proceedings for an Address in Parliament, and what the meanings of 'judicial office', 'senior judge' and 'sentence' are. It provides that 'subject to prescribed procedures' and 'under investigation for an offence' may be defined in regulations.

Section 110: Applications to the Ombudsman

320. Section 110 gives the Judicial Appointments and Conduct Ombudsman the powers to carry out a review of how a disciplinary case about a judge has been handled, at the application of an interested party, and sets out the conditions for a review. An interested party is either the judge concerned or the person, if any, who complained about his conduct. Applications for a review must be based on the grounds that those who have investigated the complaint have failed to comply with the prescribed procedures, contained in regulations made by the Lord Chief Justice under section 115 and rules made by him under section 117, or that there has been some other maladministration. The Ombudsman is not involved in reviewing the judge's conduct itself, and cannot make determinations about the merits of the decision made in a disciplinary case. For the Ombudsman to review a case, he must be satisfied that the issue is of sufficient substance for a review to be necessary. The application must have been made within the 28 days which the section prescribes, or within a time the Ombudsman considers reasonable in the circumstances, both generally and when a review is sought on the grounds that a case has taken too long to reach a conclusion. The application must be made in a form approved by the Ombudsman.

321. The section then lists the scope of the disciplinary functions which the Ombudsman will be able to investigate, which are: the exercise of the Lord Chancellor's power to remove judicial office holders as dealt with in section 108(1) of the Act; the Lord Chief Justice's new disciplinary powers dealt with in section 108(3)-(7); and any exercise of the disciplinary regulations and rules to be made by the Lord Chief Justice under section 115 and section 117.

Section 111: Review by the Ombudsman

322. Section 111 sets out the duties of the Ombudsman when carrying out a review of how a disciplinary case about a judge has been handled (in terms of alleged failure to comply with prescribed procedures or other alleged maladministration). It requires the Ombudsman to decide to what extent any application to him is justified and to make recommendations, which may include a recommendation for the payment of compensation resulting from any failure or maladministration to which the application relates. If the Ombudsman finds that the result of a disciplinary process was unreliable because of a failure to apply prescribed procedures or other procedural flaws, he will be able to set aside the decision, and require that the matter be subject to further investigation and reconsideration, in accordance with prescribed procedures. In exercising these powers, the Ombudsman will be able to direct the extent to which any previous investigation or review may be taken into account. This will mean that the whole of a previous investigation need not be disregarded if, for example, only the decision-making process at the end was procedurally flawed.

Section 112: Reports on reviews

323. Section 112 provides that, after the Ombudsman has conducted a review on an application, he must submit a report in draft to the Lord Chief Justice and the Lord Chancellor. He must have regard to any proposals they make for amendment, and if their proposals are not reflected in his final report he must include a statement of those proposals.

324. The final report must be sent separately to both the Lord Chief Justice and the Lord Chancellor. He will also send a copy of the report to the applicant, but this version is not to contain confidential information relating to someone other than the applicant.

Section 113: References to the Ombudsman relating to conduct

325.   Section 113 provides for the Lord Chief Justice or the Lord Chancellor to be able to refer to the Ombudsman any matters relating to the exercise of their disciplinary functions, either generally or in relation to particular cases. It will enable the Lord Chancellor and the Lord Chief Justice, together or separately, to ask the Ombudsman to examine aspects of the complaints handling process – if for example they had become concerned by repeated issues in a number of cases - and report to them generally.

Section 114: Reports on references

326.   Section 114 provides for the Ombudsman to report on his investigations under section 113. The report, which must be signed by the Ombudsman, will include his findings and any action he recommends. After the Ombudsman has conducted an investigation he must submit a report in draft to the Lord Chief Justice and the Lord Chancellor. He must then have regard to any proposals they make for amendment, and if their proposals are not reflected in his final report he must include a statement of those proposals. He must send the final report in duplicate to the Lord Chief Justice and the Lord Chancellor.

Section 115: Regulations about procedures

327.   Section 115 provides that the Lord Chief Justice may, with the agreement of the Lord Chancellor make regulations governing the handling of judicial disciplinary cases. These regulations will be made by statutory instrument as though they had been made by a Minister, and will (by virtue of section 144) be subject to the negative resolution procedure in Parliament. It is intended that the regulations will provide the structure of the complaints and discipline system, and will include, for example, provisions relating to the judicial investigation of serious complaints and the possibility of referring serious complaints to a review body to consider the relevant facts and allegations and advise the Lord Chief Justice and Lord Chancellor.

Section 116: Contents of regulations

328.   Section 116 provides some more detail about what regulations made by the Lord Chief Justice under section 115 may contain. These matters include the procedures to be followed; any time limits for an investigation; the persons by whom an investigation is to be conducted; the matters to be decided by the Lord Chief Justice, the Minister or anyone else; any requirements as to record-keeping and confidentiality; or any requirements as to publicity. Regulations may require the Lord Chief Justice and Minister to make their eventual decision in accordance with findings of fact made by some other person or body (such as a review body of the kind referred to in paragraphs 96 to 99 of the Concordat (as to which see paragraph 7 above)); they may require that prescribed procedural steps be taken by the Lord Chief Justice or the Minister before they can exercise their functions, or in exercising those functions. Regulations may provide for the Lord Chief Justice and Minister to disapply requirements if they both agree. Where the regulations impose a requirement on an office holder or complainant, they may provide a procedural penalty (such as suspension or dismissal of a complaint) for failure to comply.

Section 117: Procedural Rules

329.   Section 117 allows the regulations made under section 115 to provide for a more limited category of detailed procedural rules in relation to complaints and discipline to be

made by the Lord Chief Justice with the agreement of the Minister. It is envisaged that these would address the detailed matters covered by the existing protocol governing complaints against judges, which was agreed by the Lord Chancellor and the judiciary and published in 2003. These rules will not be subject to Parliamentary approval and might change from time to time, but they must be published. The rules may not include provision of the kind referred to in section 109(7) or (8) (which allow certain definitions to be prescribed) or section 116(2) or (3) (which allow the regulations to make certain provision about procedural steps in decision-making and procedural penalties).

Section 118: Extension of discipline provisions to other offices

330.   Section 118 allows the Lord Chancellor to extend the new judicial disciplinary regime by order to office holders who are not senior judges and not listed in Schedule 14. It is envisaged that this will include certain office holders, such as coroners and some tribunal members, whom the Lord Chancellor has the power to remove but who are not currently appointed by him and who are therefore not currently included in Schedule 14. Such an order can only be made with the agreement of the Lord Chief Justice and is subject to the negative approval procedure in Parliament.

Section 119: Delegation of functions

331.   Section 119 provides that the Lord Chief Justice may share the complaints caseload with other senior judges, by giving him a power to delegate the greater part of his functions in this Chapter of this Part of the Act (specifically, his functions under section 108(3) to (7), 111(2), 112 and 116(3)(b)). There are two areas which he will not be able to delegate his functions: only he will be able to give the agreement which will be needed before the Lord Chancellor removes any judicial office-holder. And he will not delegate the power to refer issues to the Ombudsman, since that is likely to involve issues of policy, involving a number of complaints.

Section 120: Scotland

332.   Section 120 provides that where a member of a tribunal with UK-wide or Great Britain-wide jurisdiction who is appointed after selection by the Judicial Appointments Commission sits wholly or mainly in Scotland it is not the Lord Chief Justice of England and Wales who will have disciplinary responsibilities in relation to him, but the Lord President of the Court of Session. In performing those functions, he will work within the procedures prescribed by the Lord Chief Justice of England and Wales, so that the same procedures apply to all members of the same tribunal; but the Lord Chief Justice will have to consult the Lord President before making the regulations containing the procedures, to make sure that any relevant provisions of Scottish law are reflected in them. The greater part of these disciplinary responsibilities (in parallel with the situation in England and Wales) may also be delegated to other senior judges in Scotland.

Section 121: Northern Ireland

333.   Section 121 provides that where a member of a tribunal with UK-wide jurisdiction who is appointed after selection by the Judicial Appointments Commission sits wholly or mainly in Northern Ireland it is not the Lord Chief Justice of England and Wales who will have disciplinary responsibilities in relation to him, but the Lord Chief Justice of Northern Ireland. These responsibilities may also be delegated to other senior judges in Northern

Ireland. In performing those functions, he will work within the procedures prescribed by the Lord Chief Justice of England and Wales, so that the same procedures apply to all members of the same tribunal; but the Lord Chief Justice will have to consult the Lord Chief Justice of Northern Ireland before making the regulations containing the procedures, to make sure that any relevant provisions of Northern Ireland law are reflected in them. The greater part of these disciplinary responsibilities (in parallel with the situation in England and Wales) may also be delegated to other senior judges in Northern Ireland.

Chapter 4: Interpretation of Part 4

Section 122: Interpretation of Part 4

334. Section 122 provides definitions of certain terms in Part 4 of the Act.

PART 5: JUDICIAL DISCIPLINE: NORTHERN IRELAND

SUMMARY

335. Part 5 amends the Justice (Northern Ireland) Act 2002 to make provision in relation to the office of the Northern Ireland Judicial Appointments Ombudsman and to provide a statutory power of disclosure of information, held by permitted persons, to the Northern Ireland Judicial Appointments Commission. It also provides for the removal of judicial office holders in Northern Ireland.

336. By virtue of section 147, Part 5 extends only to Northern Ireland.

BACKGROUND

337. The Justice (Northern Ireland) Act 2002 makes provision for the establishment of the Northern Ireland Judicial Appointments Commission ("the NIJAC"). There is no provision in that Act in relation to disclosure of information pursuant to applications for judicial appointment. In line with England and Wales, provision is made in Part 5 to provide that information held by, or on behalf of "permitted persons", may be disclosed to the NIJAC, for the purpose of selecting individuals for judicial appointment. Security and financial checks are to be carried out with a number of law-enforcement organisations, with regard to the background of individuals, before they can be appointed to judicial office.

338. Part 5 also makes provision for the establishment of the office of the Northern Ireland Judicial Appointments Ombudsman. The Ombudsman will exercise an independent external complaints function in relation to individual judicial appointments in Northern Ireland recommended by the Northern Ireland Judicial Appointments Commission. (This will be in addition to the internal procedure established by the Commission to address complaints in the first instance.) He will receive and investigate individual complaints in respect of procedural conduct of judicial appointments, where maladministration, discrimination or unfairness is alleged to have occurred during competitions for particular posts. The Ombudsman will not have a role in relation to maladministration in relation to appointments to the most senior offices (Lord Chief Justice and Lord Justice of Appeal) as appointment to those offices will not fall within the remit of Northern Ireland Judicial Appointments Commission.

339. At present, the Lord Chief Justice, Lords Justices of Appeal and High Court Judges hold office during good behaviour subject to removal by Her Majesty after an address by

Parliament. The Lord Chancellor can remove most other judicial office holders on grounds of misbehaviour or incapacity.

340.   The Justice (Northern Ireland) Act 2002, as amended by the Justice (Northern Ireland) Act 2004, makes provision for removal of judicial office holders when responsibility for judicial appointments is devolved to the Northern Ireland Assembly.

341.   Sections 133 to 136 of the Act make provision for the removal of judicial office holders on reform of the office of the Lord Chancellor, taking account of the post devolution provisions in the 2002 Act. As at present, the Lord Chief Justice, Lords Justices of Appeal and High Court judges will hold office during good behaviour and may only be removed by Her Majesty after an address by Parliament. A motion for the presentation of an address may be made to the House of Commons by the Prime Minister and to the House of Lords by the Lord Chancellor or, if the Lord Chancellor is not a member of the House of Lords, another Minister of the Crown at his request. The Act empowers the Lord Chancellor to remove judicial office holders below High Court judge level, on the ground of misbehaviour or inability to perform the functions of the office, after consultation with the Lord Chief Justice.

342.   A judicial office holder can only be removed from office following a recommendation by a removals tribunal. The Act details how such a tribunal may be convened and provides for its membership. The power to convene and the membership of a removals tribunal varies depending on the level of judge whose removal is under consideration.

COMMENTARY ON SECTIONS

Chapter 1 Appointments Commission

Disclosure of information to the Commission

Section 123: Disclosure of information to the Northern Ireland Judicial Appointments Commission

343.   The Justice (Northern Ireland) Act 2002 provides for the creation of the Northern Ireland Judicial Appointments Commission. There is currently no provision in the 2002 Act for disclosure of information, held by permitted persons, to the Commission for the purposes of selection for appointment to judicial office. This section makes provision equivalent to that made in section 107 of the Constitutional Reform Act for disclosure to the Judicial Appointments Commission in England and Wales. Permitted persons are defined as:

- a chief officer of police of a police force in England and Wales;
- a chief constable of a police force in Scotland;
- the Chief Constable of the Police Service of Northern Ireland;
- the Director General of the National Criminal Intelligence Service;
- the Director General of the National Crime Squad;
- the Commissioners of Inland Revenue; and
- the Commissioners of Customs and Excise.

344.   This section also provides that the Lord Chancellor may, by order, designate other persons who exercise functions, which he considers are of a public nature, as 'permitted persons'.

Ombudsman

Section 124: Northern Ireland Judicial Appointments Ombudsman

345.   Sections 124 to 131 amend the Justice (Northern Ireland) Act 2002 to establish the office of Judicial Appointments Ombudsman for Northern Ireland. Section 124 inserts section 9A into the 2002 Act to establish the Ombudsman's office and provide that he shall be appointed by Her Majesty the Queen on the recommendation of the Lord Chancellor.

Schedule 15: Northern Ireland Judicial Appointments Ombudsman

346.   Schedule 15 inserts Schedule 3A into the 2002 Act. Schedule 3A makes further provision in relation to the qualification, tenure of office and powers of the Ombudsman. The eligibility provisions reflect those that currently apply to the Judicial Appointments Commissioner for Northern Ireland, namely that he must not engage in political activity during the term of his appointment. Previous political activity will not constitute a bar to appointment.

Complaints and references

Section 125: Complaints: interpretation

347.   Section 125 inserts section 9B into the 2002 Act to provide an interpretation of the different types of complaint which may be made to the Ombudsman, namely a Commission complaint (where the complaint is about the Commission's handling of a candidate for judicial appointment's application) and a departmental complaint (where the complaint is about alleged maladministration by the Lord Chancellor or the Northern Ireland Court Service's handling of an application). Those entitled to complain are those who have applied for selection or have been selected for appointment to a listed judicial office, (that is, offices listed in Schedule 1 to the Justice (Northern Ireland) Act 2002, which includes the judicial office of High Court Judge and below) and claim to have been adversely affected by the maladministration about which they are complaining.

Section 126: Complaints to the Commission or the Lord Chancellor

348.   Section 126 inserts section 9C into the 2002 Act to require the Commission and the Lord Chancellor each to make arrangements for handling complaints made to them in relation to judicial appointments but provides that the arrangements need not apply to complaints made more than 28 days after the matter complained of.

Section 127: Complaints to the Ombudsman

349.   Section 127 inserts section 9D into the 2002 Act to provide that the Ombudsman must investigate any complaints relating to judicial appointments that are made within 28 days of the person concerned being notified of the Minister's or Commission's decision on their complaint unless he considers that investigation is not necessary. The Ombudsman also has discretion whether or not to investigate complaints received at any other time. Any complaint made to the Ombudsman must be in a form approved by him. This section also makes transitional provision to allow for any ongoing complaints to be transferred from the

Northern Ireland Commissioners for Judicial Appointments to the Northern Ireland Ombudsman upon the commencement of this section.

Section 128: Report and recommendations

350.   Section 128 inserts section 9E into the 2002 Act to provide that the Ombudsman must prepare a report in relation to any complaint investigated by him. In his report he may make recommendations for action to be taken by the Commission or by the Lord Chancellor, including payment of compensation (albeit that any compensation is limited to loss suffered as a result of maladministration, and not in respect of any earnings the complainant would have received had his application for appointment been successful.)

Section 129: Report procedure

351.   Section 129 inserts section 9F into the 2002 Act to provide that the Ombudsman shall send his report in draft to the Lord Chancellor, and, if the complaint related to the Judicial Appointments Commission, to the Commission also.   Before finalising the report, the Ombudsman must have regard to any proposals they make for amendment, and if their proposals are not reflected in his final report he must include a statement of those proposals. In addition to sending the finalised report to the Lord Chancellor, and where appropriate the Commission, the Ombudsman shall send a copy (which must not include confidential information) to the complainant.

Section 130: References by the Lord Chancellor

352.   Section 130 inserts section 9G into the 2002 Act to provide that the Lord Chancellor may refer to the Ombudsman any matters relating to the Commission's procedures, and for the Ombudsman to report on his investigations.

Section 131: Information

353.   Section 131 inserts section 9H into the 2002 Act to require the Commission and the Lord Chancellor to provide the Judicial Appointments Ombudsman with such information, or produce any such documentation that he may need to perform his functions in relation to complaints about judicial appointments.

Section 132: Confidentiality in relation to judicial appointments and discipline

354.   Section 132 inserts section 9I into the 2002 Act to provide that any person who obtains confidential information, or to whom confidential information is provided, under or for the purposes of any relevant provision relating to judicial appointments and discipline, must not disclose that confidential information without lawful authority.

Chapter 2: Removals

Section 133: Removal from most senior judicial offices

355.   Section 133 inserts a new section 12B in the Judicature (Northern Ireland) Act 1978 to make provision for the removal of senior judicial office holders in Northern Ireland. Her Majesty may remove the Lord Chief Justice, a Lord Justice of Appeal or a High Court judge on an address presented by both Houses of Parliament. A motion for the presentation of an address may be made to the House of Commons by the Prime Minister and to the House of Lords by the Lord Chancellor or, of the Lord Chancellor is not a member of that House, by another Minister of the Crown at his request. However, a motion for the presentation of an

address can be made only if a removals tribunal convened under section 135 of the Act (see below) has reported to the Lord Chancellor recommending removal on the ground of misbehaviour. The report must be laid before each House of Parliament. Subsection (6) of the new section 12B provides for the suspension of a senior judicial office holder while the making of motions for the presentation of an address is under consideration. The Prime Minister may suspend the Lord Chief Justice. A Lord Justice of Appeal or a High Court judge may be suspended by the Prime Minister with the agreement of the Lord Chief Justice.

Section 134: Removal from listed judicial offices

356.   Section 134 gives the Lord Chancellor the power to remove a judicial office holder below the level of High Court judge but only if a tribunal convened under section 135 of the Act (see below) has recommended removal on the ground of misbehaviour or inability to perform the functions of the office and after consultation with the Lord Chief Justice. The section also gives the Lord Chancellor the power to suspend a judicial office holder below the level of High Court judge pending a decision on their removal but only if a tribunal considering whether to recommend removal has recommended suspension and after consultation with the Lord Chief Justice.

Section 135: Tribunals for considering removal

357.   Section 135 provides for the convening of tribunals to consider the removal of holders of protected judicial office (as defined in section 136 of the Act). A tribunal to consider the removal of the Lord Chief Justice may be convened by the Lord Chancellor provided the Prime Minister has been consulted. A tribunal to consider the removal of a Lord Justice of Appeal may be convened by the Lord Chancellor after consulting the Lord Chief Justice and the Prime Minister, or by the Lord Chief Justice after consulting the Lord Chancellor and the Prime Minister. A tribunal to consider the removal of all other holders of protected judicial office may be convened by the Lord Chancellor after consulting the Lord Chief Justice, or by the Lord Chief Justice after consulting the Lord Chancellor.

358.   A tribunal will consist of three members: a judicial chairman, a judicial member and a layperson. The judicial members of a tribunal to consider the removal of the Lord Chief Justice of Northern Ireland, a Lord Justice of Appeal or a High Court judge are to be selected by the Lord Chancellor after consultation with the Lord Chief Justice of Northern Ireland (unless the tribunal is to consider his removal), the President of the Supreme Court of the United Kingdom, the Lord Chief Justice of England and Wales and the Lord President of the Court of Session. Such a tribunal will be chaired by a person who holds high judicial office (within the meaning of Part 3 of the Act) and has never been a senior judicial office holder in Northern Ireland. The other judicial member will be a current or retired judge of the Court of Appeal of England and Wales or the Inner House of the Court of Session.

359.   The judicial members of a tribunal to consider the removal of any other holder of protected judicial office are to be selected by the Lord Chief Justice and such a tribunal will be chaired by a person who holds, or has held, the office of Lord Chief Justice or Lord Justice of Appeal. The other judicial member will be a High Court judge. The lay member of a tribunal will be appointed by the Lord Chancellor.

360.   This section further provides that the procedure of a tribunal is to be determined by the Lord Chief Justice unless this office is vacant, he is unavailable or the tribunal is to

consider his removal from office, in which case the procedure is to be determined by the chairman.

Section 136: Interpretation of Part 5

361.   Section 136 defines, for the purpose of Part 5 of the Act, the meaning of "listed judicial office", "Lord Chief Justice", "Lord Justice of Appeal" and "protected judicial office".

PART 6: OTHER PROVISIONS RELATING TO THE JUDICIARY

COMMENTARY ON SECTIONS

Section 137: Parliamentary Disqualification

362.   In summary, section 137 has the effect of barring members of the Supreme Court of the United Kingdom from membership of the House of Commons and the Northern Ireland Assembly; and of barring them, and certain other holders of judicial office which exclude the holder from membership of the House of Commons, from sitting and voting in the House of Lords while they hold that office.

363.   Subsection (1) inserts the office of 'Judge of the Supreme Court' into Part 1 of Schedule 1 to the House of Commons Disqualification Act 1975. Subsection (2) makes corresponding provision for the Northern Ireland Assembly Disqualification Act 1975 (specific provision in relation to the Scottish Parliament and National Assembly for Wales being unnecessary because disqualification for membership of those bodies is tied to the House of Commons Disqualification Act).   This of itself ensures that the holders of that office are, for as long as they hold it, disqualified for membership of the House of Commons. Taken with subsection (3), this has the effect of making it impossible to hold full-time high judicial office and at the same time be an active member of the House of Lords.

364.   Subsection (3) bars holders of any "disqualifying judicial office" (defined in subsection (4) as the offices in Schedule 1 to the House of Commons Disqualification Act 1975 and the corresponding list in the Northern Ireland Assembly Disqualification Act 1975) from sitting or voting in the House of Lords or in any Lords Committee or Joint Committee. Such a person does not cease to be a member of the House while this disqualification continues, however.

365.   Subsection (3) means that a person who is disqualified from sitting and voting in the House of Lords by virtue of subsection (2) is not disqualified from receiving a writ of summons to the House of Lords.

Section 138 and Schedule 16: Judicial Committee of the Privy Council

366.   Section 138 introduces Schedule 16 which amends various statutory provisions to remove the right of the Lord President of the Council to be a member of the Judicial Committee of the Privy Council, and to sit judicially. Paragraph 2 of that Schedule recasts section 1 of the Judicial Committee Act of 1833 to redefine the membership of the Judicial Committee. This has the effect of removing not only the Lord President, but also the Lord Chancellor, Lord Keeper and Commissioners of the Great Seal. It also removes the (now in practice obsolete) power to appoint to the Judicial Committee other members of the Privy Council who do not fulfil the statutory requirements. Members of the Judicial Committee of the Privy Council from the United Kingdom will in future be only those Privy Councillors

who have held high judicial office as defined by Part 3 of the present Act (The Supreme Court). This will include judges of the new United Kingdom Supreme Court. Other enactments also provide for certain Commonwealth judges to be members of the Judicial Committee of the Privy Council. These judges' membership of the Judicial Committee is maintained Paragraph 3 of the Schedule requires the appointment of the registrar of the Judicial Committee to be made only after consultation with the President of the Supreme Court.

PART 7: GENERAL

COMMENTARY ON SECTIONS

Section 139: Confidentiality

367.   Section 139 is a general confidentiality provision which applies to the selection and appointment of Justices of the Supreme Court under sections 26 to 31 in Part 3 of the Act and to the selection, appointment and discipline of judicial office holders under Part 4 and under any regulations and rules made under Part 4. All information which relates to an identified or identifiable individual is confidential and can be disclosed only with lawful authority. Disclosure without lawful authority is made subject to a civil action for breach of statutory duty.

368.   Information may be lawfully disclosed with the consent of the person concerned; or where disclosure is necessary in order for a person to perform their functions in relation to the selection, appointment or disciplining of judicial office holders; or where disclosure is necessary in connection with the exercise of Parliamentary powers to remove a senior judge or a decision whether to exercise such powers; or where the disclosure is necessary in connection with the exercise of powers to remove, discipline or suspend a judicial office holder; or where the disclosure is required for the purposes of legal proceedings in order to comply with court rules or a court order.

369.   Where confidential information has been provided by one identifiable person about another identifiable person, it relates to both, and may only be disclosed to the subject of the information with the consent of its provider.

370.   Despite the confidentiality provisions, the Lord Chancellor and Lord Chief Justice may decide to disclose information about disciplinary action taken against an identifiable judicial office holder. Disclosure which would otherwise be prohibited by this section is also permitted if the information concerned is already available to the public from other sources, or has been so in the past.

Section 140 "Enactment"

371.   Section 140 defines "enactment" for the purposes of the Act. Different Parts of the Act extend to different parts of the United Kingdom. In those Parts of the Act that apply throughout the United Kingdom, "enactment" is defined to include Acts of the Scottish Parliament and Northern Ireland legislation. In those Parts that extend only to England and Wales and Northern Ireland, "enactment" refers only to Acts of the Westminster Parliament and Northern Ireland legislation (and, where necessary, Measures of the Church of England). The aim is to remove any uncertainty about the meaning of the term "enactment" in different Parts of the Act.

Section 141 "Subordinate Legislation"

372.   Section 141 defines "subordinate legislation" for the purposes of the Act, giving it the same meaning as in the Interpretation Act 1978, but also providing that in the context of making supplementary provisions about functions of the Lord Chancellor, and other transitional or consequential provisions, it also includes an enactment contained in an instrument made under Northern Ireland legislation.

Section 142: General Interpretation

373.   The section defines "functions" to include powers and duties, and extends the definition of "Minister of the Crown" in the Ministers of the Crown Act 1975 so that it applies in this Act.

Section 143: Supplementary provision etc

374.   Section 143 provides for the Lord Chancellor to make, by order (made by statutory instrument), any supplementary, incidental, consequential, transitory, transitional or saving provision, as he considers necessary or expedient for the purposes of the Act, in consequence of it, or to give it full effect. Subsection (2) makes it clear that such an order can, if necessary, amend or repeal other enactments, subordinate legislation, and other instruments or documents.

Section 144: Orders and Regulations

375.   Section 144 regulates the way in which the Lord Chancellor may exercise the order making powers conferred on him elsewhere in the Act. These will generally be subject to the negative resolution procedure in Parliament, except for the following, which will be subject to the affirmative resolution procedure:

- an order under section 85(2)(a) or (b) (selection of puisne judges and other office holders) that amends Part 1 of Schedule 14 (The Judicial Appointments Commission: relevant offices and enactments);

- an order under section 19(1) (transfer, modification or abolition of functions by order) which amends a public general Act, except where the only amendment is to include a function of the Lord Chancellor in Schedule 7 (protected functions of the Minister);

- an order under section 19(1) (transfer, modification or abolition of functions by order) which amends subordinate legislation of which a draft was required to be laid before and approved by each House of Parliament, except where the only amendment consists of a provision that falls within subsection 2(b) of section 19

- an order under section 143 (supplementary provision etc) which amends a public general Act;

- an order under paragraph 5 of Schedule 12 (the Judicial Appointments Commission).

376.   In addition, commencement orders made under sections 66(5) and 148 are, as usual with such instruments, not subject to Parliamentary scrutiny.

Section 145 and Schedule 17: Minor and Consequential amendments

377.   Section 145 introduces Schedule 17 which contains some minor and consequential amendments to other legislation that follow from the substantive sections of the Act.

Section 146 and Schedule 18: Repeals and revocations

378.   Section 146 introduces Schedule 18 which lists legislation repealed or revoked by, or in consequence of, other provisions in the Act.

Section 147: Extent

379.   This section sets out the territorial extent of the Act. Different parts of the Act extend to different parts of the United Kingdom. Certain provisions relating to the President of the Courts of England and Wales and the Heads and Deputy Heads of Criminal and Family Justice extend to England and Wales only. Section 6 (Representations to the Northern Ireland Assembly) and Part 5 extend to Northern Ireland alone. Amendments made by the Act will have the same extent as the provisions being amended. The Act otherwise extends to the whole of the United Kingdom.

Section 148: Commencement

380.   Provisions relating to the Speakership of the House of Lords, functions of the Lord Chancellor subject to transfer, modification or abolition, protected functions of the Lord Chancellor, interpretation, supplementary provision, ancillary provision for orders and regulations, extent, commencement and short title will come into force on Royal Assent. Section 4   (Guarantee of continued judicial independence: Northern Ireland) will be brought into force in accordance with an order made by the Secretary of State. All other provisions in the Act will be brought into force by order by the Lord Chancellor, who may make different arrangements for different purposes. Subsections (4) and (5) set out requirements relating to approval of accommodation for the Supreme Court, which must be fulfilled before the provision establishing the Supreme Court, section 23(1), may be brought into force.

EFFECTS OF THE ACT ON PUBLIC EXPENDITURE

Arrangements to modify the office of Lord Chancellor

381.   The provisions in the Act are expected to have limited financial implications. The overall staff numbers required to support those office holders to whom functions are transferred are expected to remain broadly similar to those currently required. There may, however, be some transfer of staff resources internally to reflect the new arrangements.

The Supreme Court

382.   At present, the Appellate Committee is funded through the House of Lords and its administrative support is provided by the House's administration under the Clerk of the Parliaments. Total expenditure in 2002-3 was £650,372 (£623,548 in 2001-02; £590,988 in 2000-01; £605,060 in 1999-2000). These figures include staff salaries but do not include common services in the Palace such as library, security and accommodation costs. Nor do they include the Law Lords' salaries. Total receipts from fees charged on civil but not criminal judicial business and on assessment of lawyers' bills of costs were £499,715 (£443,220 in 2000-01; £496,708 in 1999-2000; and £494,435 in 1998-99). The Judicial Committee is funded through the Privy Council office. Revised arrangements will therefore have to be made for the new Court.

383.   The cost of establishing the Supreme Court has two main elements: initial accommodation set up and annual running costs. Middlesex Guildhall on Parliament Square is the preferred option for housing the Supreme Court. This will, of course, require the

normal planning approvals and designs are under discussion with English Heritage and Westminster City Council, as well as the Lords of Appeal in Ordinary. Set up costs for refurbishing Middlesex Guildhall will be approximately £30m in current terms. This £30m estimate comprises both base costs and 'optimism bias'. The base costs are construction costs and statutory fees of £15m; £2m professional fees; and £3m VAT. Those figures are then inflated by 50% 'optimism bias' in accordance with HM Treasury guidance on financial appraisal and evaluation. However, this does not necessarily equate to the amount of capital funding that the Government will have to find; there are procurement solutions under consideration which would enable the costs to be spread across a number of years. In addition, it will be necessary to provide additional courtrooms to take on Middlesex Guildhall's Crown Court work. Provision of the additional courtrooms will cost a further £15m in current terms (including 'optimism bias'). The aim is that the first sitting of the Supreme Court would be in 2008.

384.   The approximate annual cash running costs following establishment of the Supreme Court would be £8.8m (£8.4m relating to the Supreme Court; the remainder being the ongoing costs from courtroom reprovision). This figure includes £2.1m judicial remuneration; £1.1m staff salaries; £1.0m administrative costs; £0.4m utilities and rates; and £3.8m building costs (including capital charge/lease costs and building maintenance costs) Approximately 32% of judicial remuneration and 80% of the remaining Supreme Court running costs will be recovered through fee income or through defrayment across the UK.

385.   The costs of the United Kingdom Supreme Court attributable to civil business will be recovered through fee recovery. The Supreme Court will, like the House of Lords, be the final court of appeal for all civil matters in the United Kingdom. The development of the law by the Supreme Court in the exercise of the jurisdiction transferred to it from the House of Lords and Judicial Committee of the Privy Council will be of benefit in each of the parts of the United Kingdom in the same way as is the development of the law by the House of Lords and Judicial Committee in exercising that same jurisdiction at present.

386.   The fee structure for the Supreme Court will be based upon that applicable to the Appellate Committee, but will be restructured in order to bring it into line with fee structures in the lower courts. On the basis of the running cost figures above, the total revenue for the Court is projected to amount to £6.3 million per annum.

387.   The costs of the court attributed to criminal appeals and devolution cases are likely to amount to approximately £2.1 million and will be met by direct taxation via the Department for Constitutional Affairs vote.

Judicial Appointments Commission

388.   At present the Judicial Appointments Directorate is funded through the Department of Constitutional Affairs' vote. The Judicial Appointments Commission will be funded via grant-in-aid also through the Department for Constitutional Affairs vote.

389.   The cost of establishing the Judicial Appointments Commission is estimated to be £3.2 million. This is based on the Commission being located within existing Department of Constitutional Affairs estate in the early part of its life. These set up costs for the Commission will be split over three financial years. £0.2m in 2003-4 and £0.37m in 2004-5 costs preparing for implementation have already been incurred, and the remainder of set up costs will be incurred in2005/2006. There are also plans for the greater part of the

Commission to relocate out of London and the South east in 2008, leaving it with twin locations. Estimated costs for this relocation are in the region of £1.7 million.

390.   The annual running cost of the Commission has been estimated at approximately £8.5 million, reducing to £8 million in 2007/2008, due to its partial relocation of out of London and the Southeast. Approximately £2 million of this running cost is attributable to indirect costs such as accommodation, and the remainder of the costs will be the "running costs" of the Commission. The actual running cost of the appointment process will be in the region of £5.5 million of which £4.2 million will be spent on salaries. It is estimated that the cost of the Commissioners will be £665,000 per annum.

The Judicial Appointments and Conduct Ombudsman

391.   The Ombudsman will be funded through the Department for Constitutional Affairs' vote as it is likely to be an associated office of the Department for Constitutional Affairs.

392.   The cost of establishing the Ombudsman office will be approximately £0.4m. £0.06m was incurred in 2004-5 and the remainder will be incurred in 2005-6

393.   The maximum annual cost of running the Ombudsman's office will be £1.4m. This is dependent on whether the Ombudsman is based in existing Department of Constitutional Affairs estate or landlord serviced estate. The cost mentioned above is based on the Ombudsman being located in a landlord serviced building. The current Commission for Judicial Appointments, which currently carries out a part of the function that will be covered by the Ombudsman, costs the Department of Constitutional Affairs approximately £340k per annum. The Commission for Judicial Appointments is based in Department for Constitutional Affairs estate.

PUBLIC SECTOR MANPOWER

The Supreme Court

394.   The Supreme Court will be administered as a distinct constitutional entity with special funding arrangements to reflect its unique status. The staff will, however, be civil servants. The existing staff of the Judicial Office of the House of Lords have been given the opportunity to transfer to the new court and they will be supplemented by recruited staff to fill the role of those employed by the wider House and shared with the Judicial Office. At present, 21 staff are dedicated to the Judicial Office at a cost of £0.6 million. It is estimated that a further 20 posts will need to be created to fill the role of those shared with the wider House, at a cost of £0.5 million. In addition, a Chief Executive will be appointed through fair and open competition.

The Judicial Appointments Commission

395.   The effects on public service manpower will be minimal for the Judicial Appointments Commission. The Commission will be an executive Non-Departmental Public Body sponsored by the Department for Constitutional Affairs. The Commission will be staffed by a combination of new recruits, and transferred or seconded staff from the Department of Constitutional Affairs. It is estimated that the Judicial Appointments Commission will have approximately 140 staff.

The Judicial Appointments and Conduct Ombudsman

396.   The Ombudsman's office will have a minimal effect on public service manpower and will be staffed by existing civil servants from the Department of Constitutional Affairs. The estimated workload of the Ombudsman's office is still under evaluation but it is thought that there will be a need for between 6 and 14 staff.

COST TO BUSINESS AND REGULATORY IMPACT

397.   The only provision in the Act which will result in a slight increase in cost to business, charities or the voluntary sector are those in respect of the Supreme Court. The Regulatory Impact Assessments will be placed in the Library of the House and on the Department's website as accompanying documentation.

Supreme Court

398.   The Regulatory Impact Assessment (RIA) on the Supreme Court considers that there is a negligible impact on small businesses, charities and the voluntary sector. It further considers that there will be a limited impact on public and private expenditure as the majority of the costs will be defrayed across the wider civil jurisdictions from which cases come from.

399.   The RIA considers options instead of statute to create the United Kingdom Supreme Court and concludes that primary legislation is the only viable way to transfer the necessary jurisdictions.

EUROPEAN CONVENTION ON HUMAN RIGHTS

400.   Convention issues do not arise in relation to any specific provisions in the Constitutional Reform Act. The Act is in seven parts.

401.   Part 2 modifies the office of the Lord Chancellor and provides for the transfer and future exercise of certain functions presently vested in that office. The treatment of the Lord Chancellor's functions differs according to whether they are of a legislative, executive or judicial character. This part also confers a duty on Ministers of the Crown generally and particular duties on the Lord Chancellor to uphold the independence of the judiciary.

402.   The balance struck in this Part of the Act between the separation of powers and the need for democratic accountability does not infringe the ECHR, and in particular, Article 6. In the most sensitive matters (such as the discipline and removal of Judges) the concurrence of the Lord Chief Justice will act as a crucial counterweight to the powers of the Lord Chancellor. In general, the degree of autonomy of the judiciary combined with procedural checks and balances such as this, will ensure that the independence and impartiality of the judiciary will be preserved as required by Article 6.

403.   Part 3 contains provisions for the creation, constitution, jurisdiction and resourcing of a new Supreme Court for the United Kingdom. The new court will exercise the existing appellate jurisdiction of the House of Lords (the Appellate Committee) and the jurisdiction of the Judicial Committee of the Privy Council in respect of devolution issues under the Scotland Act 1998, the Government of Wales Act 1998 and the Northern Ireland Act 1998.

404.   The arrangements are considered to be sufficient to entrench and safeguard judicial independence as required by Article 6, and to prevent any legitimate or objectively-justified fear of a lack of impartiality on the part of those coming before the new Supreme Court.

405. Part 4 creates a new system for the appointment of judges in England and Wales, and for the appointment of those persons holding office of a judicial nature in England, Scotland and Wales who are currently appointed by the Lord Chancellor. The Part also makes provision for the creation of a judicial ombudsman, with responsibility for dealing with complaints about the appointment process and sets out the framework for judicial discipline.

406. Although it is not legally binding on questions of compatibility, these provisions have regard to the Council of Europe Committee of Ministers Recommendation No. R(94) 12 on the Independence, Efficiency and Role of Judges (adopted on 13th October 1994). That Recommendation states that judicial appointments should be made by a body independent of government and the administration. However, it also states that where national constitutional or legal provisions and traditions allow judges to be appointed by the government, there should be guarantees to ensure that the procedures to appoint judges are transparent and independent in practice and that the decisions will not be influenced by any reasons other than those related to objective criteria. The Recommendation goes on to state that these guarantees could take the form of a special independent and competent body to give the government advice which it follows in practice, and/or the right for an individual to appeal against a decision to an independent authority. The provisions are considered to be drafted in such a way as to ensure that the Judicial Appointments Commission will be an independent and competent body of the kind described in the Recommendation, and the process of review by the ombudsman will be a limited form of appeal to an independent authority.

407. Part 6 removes the right of the Lord President of the Council to sit judicially. This removes a potential incompatibility with the ECHR, which could arise out of a Minister sitting as a judge.

408. No specific sections in any of these Parts give rise to particular issues under the convention.

HANSARD REFERENCES

409. The following table sets out the dates and Hansard references for each stage of this Act's passage through Parliament.

Stage	Date	Hansard reference
House of Lords		
Introduction	24 February 2004	Vol 658 Col 120
Second Reading (and motion to commit the Bill to a Select Committee)	8 March 2004	Vol 658 Cols 979-1006, 1023- 1112
Select Committee Final Report presented to the HOL	24 June 2004	Vol 662 Col 1462
Committee (on the floor of the House)	13 July 2004	Vol 663 Cols 1137 – 1194, 1213-1236
	14 July 2004	Vol 663 Cols 1297 – 1350

	11 October 2004	Vol 665 Cols 12 – 76, 89 - 110
	18 October 2004	Vol 665 Cols 527- 542, 567-602, 619, 642
Report	7 December 2004	Vol 667 Cols 738 –812, 818- 892
	14 December 2004	Vol 667 Cols 1180- 1257, 1275-1322
Third Reading	20 December 2004	Vol 667 Cols 1535-1573, 1596-1625
House of Commons		
Introduction	21 December 2004	
Second Reading	17 January 2005	Vol 429 Cols 554 - 663
Committee (on the floor of the House)	31 January 2005	Vol 430 Cols 589 – 685
	1 February 2005	Vol 430 Cols 717 – 809
Report	1 March 2005	Vol 431 Cols 822 - 928
Third Reading	1 March 2005	Vol 431 Cols 822 - 928
Lords Consideration of Commons Amendments	15 March 2005	Vol 670 Cols 1211 - 1275
Commons Consideration of Lords Amendments	16 March 2005	Vol 432 Cols 358-374
Lords Consideration of Commons Amendments	21 March 2005	Vol 671 Cols 12- 45

Royal Assent – 24 March 2005   House of Lords Hansard Vol. 671 Col 412
House of Commons Hansard Vol. 432 Col 1036

Printed in the UK by The Stationery Office Limited
under the authority and superintendence of Carol Tullo, Controller of
Her Majesty's Stationery Office and Queen's Printer of Acts of Parliament.

7/2005   311035   19585